A Way in to the Trinity

Inigo Texts Series: 7

A Way in to the Trinity

The story of a journey

Gerald O'Mahony, SJ

GRACEWING

First published in 2004

Gracewing   Inigo Enterprises
2 Southern Avenue   Links View, Traps Lane
Leominster   and   New Malden
Herefordshire HR6 0QF   Surrey KT3 4RY

Cover picture: *Holy Island from Lamlash* by Craigie Aitchison
(1994), by kind permission of the artist.

ISBN 0 85244 591 1

Typesetting by
Action Publishing Technology Ltd, Gloucester GL1 5SR

CONTENTS

List of Diagrams   ix
Preface *by Father Billy Hewett, SJ*   xi
Foreword *by Father Gerard W. Hughes, SJ*   xii

Introduction   xv
    Fulfilment of long-standing desire • Not a technical
    book but a book about a lifetime's personal
    relationship to God as Trinity • Closely connected
    with the Good News, which must be preached.

Chapter 1: Age 1–11   1
    First memories of 'Holy God' friendly • Separation
    from parents for 8 months • Primary school, Jesus,
    catechism mostly bad, some parts good • Enormous
    fear taught along with first confession and first
    Communion • Taught to converse with Jesus.

Chapter 2: Age 11–20   9
    Secondary school years • Confirmation, Holy Spirit
    • Thérèse of Lisieux • 'Schizophrenia' continues but
    less severe • Jesuit Noviceship entered • Spiritual
    Exercises of St Ignatius • Fr Clifford Howell •
    Frank Sheed • Two 'consolations without previous
    cause' give courage.

Chapter 3: Age 20–29   19
   Juniorate year in London • 'For whose sake?'
   • Rublev icon (i) • Philosophy • 'In God no
   might-have-beens' (i) • Trinity and Fifth Station of
   the Cross • Breakdown • 'Eternal forgiveness'
   experience • Teaching, then theology in Dublin
   • Sermon on the Trinity • Trinity foreshadowed in
   the Old Testament?

Chapter 4: Age 30–40   28
   Ordination, fourth year of theology • Through
   St Mark, theology matches experience • The Spirit
   coming with love and the Spirit leading into love
   • Faith the beginning, love the end • Bread and
   water, then wine(i) • Love-with-no-strings from God,
   and the response is gratitude • Two-faceted images,
   namely fire, water, rock, tree, wind and bread
   • 'Outside the city'.

Chapter 5: Age 40–50   39
   Advisor to religious education teachers, Liverpool
   • Redemption, why did Jesus have to die? • God
   our Saviour and 'Abba' • Baptism, confirmation,
   reconciliation, original sin, Eucharist re-presenting
   death and Resurrection • Martin Luther • Being one
   with Jesus on the Cross (as since Tertianship) • The
   start of writing books – my own catechism, junior
   syllabus, *Seventy Times Seven* and the germ of *The
   Two-Edged Gospel* • Invited to be Novice Director •
   Short lived as such, then another breakdown.

Chapter 6: Age 50–55   50
   Breakdown to breakthrough • Bread, water and
   wine (ii) • 'The other side of the mountain' reached
   in seven stages • 'Father' or 'Our Father' – which
   comes first? • Rublev icon of the Trinity (ii) •
   'Nearest to the heart' • 'Through Christ our Lord'
   • Rembrandt pictures Trinity.

Chapter 7: Age 56–59   62
Scale of moods noticed and written up • Link with
Trinity • Leads in to noticing and researching two
sides of the Gospel • Link with Holy Spirit •
Awareness of God within, looking out • Loneliness
never necessary • God's full attention • God has no
favourites.

Chapter 8: Age 60–62   72
The question of 'he' and 'she' and 'it' and God •
First Person, the love that nobody loved first •
Second Person, love-in-return-for-that-love, begotten
by that love • Third Person, communication of that
love, in the two directions • Julian of Norwich,
creator, wisdom, love, God the Father, God the
Mother, God the Lord of love • All apart from the
first unconditional love are in the role of mother,
brother, sister, not father.

Chapter 9: Age 63–64   82
Different ways of saying the same things about
spiritual progress • Classic versions in three stages
• The hosepipe! • Creation and re-creation • Bread,
water and wine again (iii) • Re-creation in Mark's
Gospel • Always designed to be children, or adopted
children?

Chapter 10: Age 65–66   92
Sharing a window on the world with God as cure for
loneliness • Impetus for Jesus' church comes from
the one to the many, from realizing oneself loved to
wanting to share the love • As also in the Trinity
• God is simple • With God no might-have-beens
(ii) • 'God is never angry' • The fruit God looks for
• More thoughts on Jesus killed 'outside the city'
• Evil and suffering and God who is love.

Chapter 11, Age 67–68   104
    Summary, favourite sentence • Elizabeth of the
    Trinity • 'God' used as meaning Son, Spirit or
    Trinity, as well as more usually Father • Selflessness
    of the First Person • Forgiveness built in to the
    Trinity itself • Where my story has reached now.

Appendix: The theology of the Trinity   116
Some books I have found useful   120

DIAGRAMS

		page
(i)	The direction in which the Spirit moves	109
(ii)	'Seven Mansions'	110
(iii)	Unquestioning love	111
(iv)	The scale of moods	112
(v)	The two sides of the Gospel	113
(vi)	Progress three stages	114
(vi)	Bread, water, wine	115
	Appendix: the theology of the Trinity	116

PREFACE

Gerry O'Mahony has already proved his worth and value in a number of shorter works referred to in the text and in the appendix. Now this book, his first larger scale publication, makes a very appropriate addition to the growing list of titles brought out jointly by Inigo Enterprises and Gracewing Publishing.

Although some books may not fit readily into some publishers' current categories, Inigo Enterprises exists to facilitate publication of just such titles. Inigo Enterprises is primarily concerned with adapting Ignatian spirituality to the signs and needs of the times, and *A Way in to the Trinity* admirably realizes this goal.

Gerry O'Mahony has the gift of linking his personal story to his personal beliefs. This is one of the great hallmarks of Ignatian spirituality, continuing the line started by Ignatius himself in his Autobiography/Testament: built into the telling of his own story is his personal witness to the specific ways in which God was shaping it at every stage. This style is highly evocative – as many contemporary as well as traditional autobiographies continue to demonstrate. Gerry O'Mahony's book will surely prove a profound and exciting addition to the genre and thus more than earns its place as an Inigo Enterprise in its own right.

Billy Hewett, SJ
Director, Inigo Enterprises

FOREWORD

Belief in the Trinity is central to the Christian Faith. Our Christian beliefs are truths, not only about God, but also about ourselves, and they are presented to help us understand the meaning, purpose and direction that our lives should take.

The Trinity, being a mystery, can never be fully understood. When theologians, teachers and preachers begin speaking of the Trinity, most of us remain totally baffled and wonder what all this complicated terminology has to do with anything on earth. We accept the Trinity as utter mystery and are pleased to let it remain so.

Gerald O'Mahony's *Way in to the Trinity* is rooted in story, the story of his own life and growth in faith, a unique, most moving, deep and wonderful story but, as he himself writes, this uniqueness is true of every human story if we learn how to look at it.

I have never read anything on the Trinity which is as life-giving as this book. The mystery, instead of appearing unintelligible and better left alone, remains mystery, but becomes something exciting, energizing, a source of life, the source of our own lives, which can never be exhausted by any amount of exploration.

The theme of the book is the unconditional love of God which is poured out on every human being – inviting, but not demanding – an unconditional response. The love poured out on Jesus is being given to us freely and continuously, even when we are unconscious of it, or reject it.

The life of God is a life of total giving between Father, Son and Holy Spirit and that is the community in which we live, move and have our being. The Trinity is not primarily a doctrine, not something we learn or come to know: it is the heart of the reality in which we live.

The content of Gerald O'Mahony's book comes out of the crucible of his own painful experience. *A Way in to the Trinity* summarizes and expands on his earlier writings. In an appendix he gives a brief theology of the Trinity as it has appeared in the Councils of the Church. Like his Lord, Gerald O'Mahony makes the dead bones live! He also provides most useful illustrations which enable readers to link what he writes with their own felt experience.

I hope and pray that this book will have a large circulation.

Gerard W. Hughes, SJ

INTRODUCTION

For years I have wanted to write a book about the Trinity, the Three Persons in the One God. Already the mystery of the Trinity has featured in just about every book or article I have ever written (and there are many of those), but for a long time it has seemed a good idea to extract all I have written about the Trinity and put it in a separate book one day. Many of the thoughts and ideas I have already featured in the past might not have seemed to be anything to do with the Trinity, but I hope that when they are selected and put side by side, they will be seen to be highly relevant to the central mystery.

The next question was, what kind of format to use in such a book? If I were to write a tome, taking the rest of my life about it, most likely it would not come up to the exacting standards of professional theology even when I had finished it, so the labour would be lost. Instead I have decided to tell what I know like a story, going through the years of my life and showing how the mystery of the Trinity meant more and more to me as each decade of my life went by. Towards the further end of my life the decades will contain too much for a single chapter, so I will take the story five years or less at a time. This will not be the complete faith story of my life, which I have already written elsewhere, but will concentrate on the way the beauty of the

Trinity has drawn me ever closer in love. I will of course check everything I write against the teachings of the Church in her Councils, to make sure I am not leading anyone astray from the ancient faith.

I have placed some diagrams at the end of the book. St Patrick could have his shamrock, Rublev could have his icon, Augustine could have his 'memory, understanding and will'; anybody who talks about the Trinity gropes around for illustrations. My diagrams are not meant to be diagrams of the Trinity: they are there to try and make clear what I myself am trying to say about the Trinity. I have also included an Appendix to relate my word-pictures to the traditional language of Western theology.

For the past forty years the main theme of all my writing and preaching and teaching has been the Good News. There seems to me little profit in discussing a thousand other things at great length when the vast majority of the human race has not yet heard the news which Jesus died to tell us. What is the Good News? It is the news that Jesus is Son of God, and that Jesus invites us to believe that we are his younger sisters and brothers. In other words, we are invited to share in the love and life of the Trinity. It follows that we are invited to understand the Trinity to the best of our ability, so as to appreciate the way God is and the way God works. In that way we will grow into our inheritance, rather than have it come as a total surprise when our days are over and we can do no more about getting ready for it, no more about living in anticipation of it.

There is a story told by Jesus in Luke's Gospel (Luke 16:19–31) about a rich man who all his life completely ignored the poor man Lazarus at his gate, and who later suffered in consequence. When I was very young I saw that story as a threat, but now for many years I have seen it rather as an invitation. Here am I, blessed with many riches, and I have the chance to share my treasures with whoever lies at the gate of my senses, whoever I come across in other words. In my life one thing I do seem to be good at is showing how simple complicated-sounding truths really are. My journey into the Trinity is obviously not over yet, but if I can share some of my wonder at the beauty of it all, then perhaps some others may be encouraged to explore their own relationship with God as being a relationship with the Trinity. They will find as I did when these truths were shared with me, that the truths about God have a way of healing the sores with which every poor Lazarus is afflicted, including the Lazarus hidden inside the rich man himself.

Chapter One

AGE 1–11

My first memories of God are of someone very friendly. As far as I remember, there was only one person involved in being God for the first five or six years of my life, namely the one I now think of as the Father of Jesus. The name of this person was 'Holy God', and that was how you spoke to him. Somewhere very early on I was taught, presumably by my mother but my father certainly went along with it, that God was all over the place, wherever you could possibly go to. Also that you could speak to Holy God in your heart with words that nobody else could hear.

Because Holy God was everywhere in the world and the stars, and yet was so close to me, I did have this desire at some future date in heaven to be taken on a tour by Holy God of every inch of the universe. He would show me how everything worked and how he made it. It would be a personal tour, one-to-one. I must also have gathered that in eternity there would be no hurry about anything, and that God could take me on a complete and leisurely tour without causing anyone else any inconvenience through his absence. Also I suspect this was my personal solution to the panic feelings I felt and have since often felt in my later life, because of the enormous size of reality and the smallness of myself: it was good that Someone knew what it was all about and how it all worked, and that the same Someone was kindly disposed towards myself.

I have sometimes wondered if the way I was taught to speak to God as 'Holy God' had some connection with the city of Cork in the south of Ireland. My parents both came from Cork, my father from Coachford in County Cork and my mother from Cork city. I discovered much later that somewhere back in the nineteenth century there was a little girl who lived there and died at the age of five who was known as (would you believe it) Little Nelly of Holy God, and there was a bit of fuss trying to get her canonized some day. It didn't come to anything. But maybe in Cork all the children at that time called God 'Holy God', and my parents caught that way of speaking about God. I do know that our mother did not like us ever speaking about 'God', just like that, as it reminded her too much of people swearing.

I was born in Wigan, in Lancashire, the youngest of three children. We were on holiday in Ireland when the Second World War broke out on 3 September 1939, and our parents left us there for a few months in Cork with our grandparents and an uncle and aunt, till it became clearer which way the war seemed to be going. One result of this was that I managed to avoid going to school till I was back in England and already turned six years old. So my idyll with Holy God lasted all that time. No doubt another result of being evacuated or exiled at the age of five was that I was suddenly made more aware of the parents I was missing so badly. I used to howl tearless howls when I was put to bed, until my auntie-cum-godmother came upstairs to calm me down, stroking my eyelashes, I remember. Holy God was no substitute for my parents at that stage of my life.

I may have heard the name Holy Spirit but it did not impinge on my mind at all. Even Jesus I cannot remember having any place in my life before I started school. I am sure I must have been told about Jesus at Christmas time, and I am sure I was taken into churches and told about Jesus in the tabernacle, but Jesus was not someone I spoke to in my heart. He came under the general aura of holy things and people, but did not figure as a real person in my life.

Primary school brought about many serious changes in my relations with God, mostly bad but some of them good. The bad and the good both came from the *Catechism of Christian Doctrine* which we had to learn by heart at school, and which was the be-all and end-all of Christian instruction among Catholics in England in those days. Let me list some of the bad things about that catechism. It said I had to save my own soul or else go to hell when I died. (I was to be twenty-four years old and on the other side of a most painful mental breakdown before I learned that, on the contrary, I cannot save my own soul, since God alone can do that.)

According to the *Catechism*, to save my soul I had to worship God by faith, hope and charity (Question 8). 'Faith' meant I had to believe the answers to the next series of questions, namely Questions 9 to 134. 'Hope' meant I had to make good use of grace, do lots of good works, and pray, especially the *Our Father* and the *Hail Mary*. That took up Questions 135 to 168. Then 'Charity' meant keeping the commandments of God and of the Church, plus the absolute need to use the sacraments, to avoid the vices, to keep the Christian's rule of life and do the daily exercises as a Christian should. All that was in Questions 169 to 370. The net result for a sensitive child such as I certainly was, was that I had 370–8 = 362 things to remember or to do every day in order to save my soul and keep away from hell when I died. One of the children in my class got run over and killed on the way home from school, Jean Perch was the little girl's name; so even then I knew life was fragile: hence hell might not be so far away. The rest of the children may have managed to keep all this in some separate compartment of their minds and carry on quite happily, but over the last sixty years I have come across hundreds of sensitive people, including some of my classmates, who have either given the whole thing up or suffered serious upset or even breakdowns because of the amount of untruth we were taught from an early age.

One way or another, that *Catechism* was certainly a Pelagian document, riddled with the Pelagian heresy which says that my salvation depends ultimately on me. If when I do die that dreadful little book is found among my possessions, let no one think this is because I had a secret love for it. I have kept it till today so as to be able to prove to anyone who says 'It wasn't as bad as all that', that it *was* as bad as all that, by being able to point to the actual wording of the fatal answers. I shall not list them all here, but I will probably bring some of them into my present story about the Trinity from time to time, as we come to the years when I learned to see the truth was other than I had been taught.

Not even the *Catechism* could get everything wrong. Rather like the curate's bad egg in the old *Punch* cartoon, parts of it were excellent, especially for budding theologians. There were lots of things in it that I found interesting and uplifting, once I could forget about the threats printed alongside. The virtues were interesting, and the vices, in an academic sort of way (the teachers got around the meaning of adultery by saying it was something adults did, and we would understand later!), and to know how many sacraments there were, and what were the gifts and the fruits of the Holy Spirit and lots of systems like that. One of the systems was how the Trinity worked, and I found that very interesting. We must have come to it pretty quickly, because the Trinity is dealt with in Questions 16 to 30, along with the beginning of the Creed in the 'faith' section.

By the time we reached the answer to Question 30, we had learnt to repeat that God made me; that God made me to know him, love him and serve him in this world, and to be happy with him for ever in the next (that was Question 2, before we discovered in Question 8 that it all depended on our own behaviour); that God made me to his own image and likeness; that God is the very truth; that God the Father Almighty is creator of heaven and earth; that God is the supreme spirit, who alone exists of himself; that he can do all things; that he made heaven and earth and all things out of nothing by his word; that he had no beginning, and that God is everywhere.

To the question 'Does God know and see all things?', the answer was, 'God knows and sees all things, even our most secret thoughts.' I remember not caring for that one much, as I would have preferred if God could only see what I told him about. God, the next answer went on, has no body; he is a spirit. There is only one God. There are three Persons in God: God the Father, God the Son, and God the Holy Ghost. The edition of my copy of the *Catechism* I keep today is as old as I am, so in those days we still spoke about the Holy Ghost rather than the Holy Spirit. That gave the teachers some problems with small children, as I can remember, small children being naturally afraid of ghosts as a general rule. Then, these three Persons were not three Gods, but all three were one and the same God. That was a mystery, and the mystery was called the mystery of the Blessed Trinity. A mystery was a truth which is above reason, but revealed by God.

The final Questions in this section, numbers 29 and 30, told us something I now know comes from St Augustine of Hippo, who saw a likeness in our human spirit to the three-in-oneness of the Trinity, because we have in our one spirit a memory, an understanding and a will. All that about God and the Trinity was a lot for little mites of six years old to fathom, and it was only the beginning. But it was certainly interesting, and not threatening in itself.

Pretty soon in school I was being prepared for my first Holy Communion. With having missed the first year in the school, I was put in a special group of those who needed to catch up with the rest of the pupils of that year. There I was told about how much Jesus loved me, and wanted to come to me in communion, and how from now on I would join the serious Christians: this was a kind of initiation into grown-up things. Jesus began to take the forefront in my spiritual thinking while the Father, or 'Holy God' went into the background. What is more, the Father became largely an object of dread, since Jesus seemed to be saving me from this hell which could only have its source in God. On the other hand, even Jesus himself was not entirely to be trusted.

For one thing, Jesus in communion only stayed around for a while, then we were on our own again, unless we called on him specially with formal prayers. More to the point, we were also being prepared for our first confession, as it was then called, and that was a minefield capable even of destroying what trust we had in Jesus as our saviour. Again it was the sensitive ones who suffered most. I can remember agonizing over whether I had lied to the Holy Ghost by not telling everything, or not telling it properly. Not at the first confession, you understand, when we were monitored and rehearsed, but afterwards, Yes.

Along with preparation for first confession we were given an enormous fear of hell, such a fear as to be paralysing. The first explicit mention of hell in the *Catechism* came at Question 74, in the article of the Creed about Christ coming to judge the living and the dead. Hell had been there implicitly from Question 8, since it was what would happen if I did not succeed in saving my soul. But then the *Catechism* really went to town on the subject of hell, sadly enough, in the article of the Apostles Creed which says 'I believe in the forgiveness of sins'. The memory of how hell was thus made to dominate forgiveness makes me really angry when I think back now. '*Question* 125: Where will they go who die in mortal sin? *Answer:* They who die in mortal sin will go to hell for all eternity.' Along with that, we were told that though baptism had given us a shiny white robe for our souls, every time we sinned we put a dirty mark on it, that only a good confession could wash off.

Add to that, lots of peccadilloes or no-sins-at-all (like whether we had swallowed some toothpaste washing our teeth when we should have been fasting before communion) this and many many more were magnified by us children into mortal sins. I for one was frequently on the brink of hell in my own mind, waiting anxiously to get to confession before I might die. Please do not think I am exaggerating: I was a very bright child and I have a very good memory. I can remember time and again on a Saturday walking or cycling across the fields to St James' church and Father Baybutt for confession. The larks would be singing, and I would say up to them 'All right for you to be singing; you've not got a load like mine on your heart!' Then on the way back I would sing along with the lark, and all would be well for a few days, until the next supposed mortal sin came along.

Father Baybutt was all right; he was very kind. The teachers were all right as well; *they* were very kind. At least they meant well. Their kindness did a lot to belie the awful travesty of the Gospel they were teaching us. If God was really like Mrs X or Miss Y, then perhaps the reality was not quite as horrific as the way they were describing it. If they really believed it was as they described things to us, they would have run away screaming long ago. Therefore there must be a better way of understanding this religion. But what?

One teacher I hero-worshipped: her name was Miss Higham: Joan Higham. She was my form teacher when I was in the class going from age ten to eleven, and she inspired me. On the question of religion, there is just one thing she said that has stayed with me ever since. She suggested that we spend a lot of wasted energy talking to ourselves. We could turn it into real energy by tacking 'Jesus' on to the end of every sentence we spoke to ourselves, then we would find we were talking to a real other person. 'The lark up there is singing ... Jesus.' 'I'm feeling tired, Jesus.' And so on, any time of any day.

I did that for forty years, and only stopped then to alter 'Jesus' to 'Father', so what Joan Higham suggested is with me still. There in my eleventh year she gave me back the same intimacy with Jesus which I had had with the Father, 'Holy God', as a little child. It was a rather schizophrenic intimacy, I must admit, since it was not entirely clear which side Jesus was on all the time, sharing my most intimate thoughts and yet apparently doomed to send me to hell if I did not finally shape up. But the intimacy was there, and has never deserted me from that day to this. The schizophrenia has been resolved along the way, but it took a long time, as I shall go on to describe.

But before I leave my memories of these years of primary school age, there is one other incident to mention that now seems to me to be significant. It was only a visit to the cinema, and the film was only *Lassie Come Home*, about a beautiful collie sheepdog that was kidnapped hundreds of miles from her Scottish home farm, and the little boy owner who missed her sadly. Through countless adventures Lassie eventually found her way home. I was deeply moved by the whole story. Maybe it all touched something deep inside me because I had been away from home for six months and was now enjoying the safety of home. Or maybe it touched something deeper still.

Chapter Two

AGE 11–20

This chapter will deal with my years at boarding school, from the age of eleven to eighteen, and then my two years as a Jesuit novice which followed straight after schooldays. For my secondary schooldays I had a year at Barlborough Hall preparatory school, then six years at Mount St Mary's College near Sheffield, which is still going strong at the present time of writing.

The fact that the Trinity was a mystery never stopped me from trying to solve the mystery. Some of my contemporaries in the Catholic Church have felt that the answer I quoted above to the question 'What is a mystery?' rather blocked them off from thinking further. The truth was seemingly 'beyond reason', so why bother trying to figure it out? Perhaps some teachers were inclined to fob off awkward questions from pupils by saying 'Oh, it's a mystery; don't expect me to explain it to you,' or words to that effect. But for my part I certainly continued in secondary school to be puzzled by the mysteries, as well as to worry about the threats there seemed to be in religion.

When I was thinking specifically about the Trinity I began to puzzle over some of the words of John's Gospel describing the discourse of Jesus at the Last Supper. 'I and the Father are one', and 'I will send the Spirit', and 'The Father will send the Spirit' and about the Spirit knowing all

the thoughts of Father and Son. The Mass which we
attended each day at boarding school was in Latin, but I
had a daily missal with translations; so between that and
sermons and places where the Gospels came into our religion lessons, we got a certain amount of exposure to the
actual words of the Gospels. I do know that when I began
to see the light about John's words on the Trinity, later, at
the age of twenty-three, I had been puzzling about them for
a very long time.

The onset of adolescence made for even more incidents
that could be thought of as mortal sins. There is still a
frequently held notion among Catholics that (according to
what they were taught at school) there can be no venial sins
against the sixth and ninth commandments. In Catholic
notation that meant those of the ten commandments of
Moses which were about adultery and lust. No such thing
as a sexual sin easily pardonable, every single one was
regarded as major, mortal, hell-worthy if you died without
confession. There was an escape-clause about making an
act of perfect contrition, which acted as a temporary solution, but as you never knew whether your act of contrition
was really perfect or not, you still had to go to confession
to make sure.

So if as an adolescent I was getting sexual thoughts all
day long which were highly attractive, where was the
borderline beyond which a thought in my head and heart
became a mortal sin? There were no larks in the sky over-
head that I can remember from the fields round Mount St
Mary's, but if there had been I know what I would have
been saying to them through most of my secondary school
days: 'All right for you feeling so blythe and happy ... etc.'
Luckily there was plenty going on at school, so there was
not much time to feel sorry for myself. The busy regime was
invented to keep our thoughts pure, I am fairly certain;
what it did for me was to keep my thoughts for the most
part away from whether I had committed another mortal
sin or not.

When I was fifteen the local bishop came to the school

and I was confirmed. What should have been a happy occasion full of hope and the Holy Spirit was for me a bundle of serious anxieties. I can remember being so worried about whether I was in a state of mortal sin, that I got one of the priest teachers to hear my confession specially an hour or so before the ceremony. Poor man, he did his best with me. All the priests who heard confessions at the school were very kind, but the damage was deep-seated and had been done in primary school.

All in all, I did not learn very much about the Holy Spirit or the Holy Ghost from that occasion. As far as I remember, the lessons in preparation for this sacrament of confirmation left me with a good picture of the Spirit, even if a limited one: the Spirit was like a breeze, to animate, to fan the flames, to make you feel like doing great things for God. The strange notions about sin I had gathered from primary school put the damper on everything, but at fifteen there was the desire to get to grips with the Spirit if only I could find peace of mind to do so.

Looking back, I would say that the things at school which really brought me closer to the Holy Spirit were the music and art appreciation hours, the training for the elocution and the essay writing competitions, the singing in the choir, the debating society, the cross-country runs, taking part in class plays, and my piano lessons. The music teacher, Harry Bruce, was to me a foretaste of the Good News, in that he was very interesting, a splendid musician – he opened up a whole world of beautiful modern music for me – he encouraged my aspirations but he never pushed me beyond where I was ready to go.

From the start at Mount St Mary's I did find some elements of religion that were gentle and helpful towards countering the fear of hell in me. There was a beautiful statue of Mary the mother of Jesus which was a focus for devotion to Mary as our mother. I was in need of a mother there at boarding school, and confided in Mary quite a lot. Then too there was frequent mention of Jesus as The Sacred Heart, and things that St Margaret Mary Alocoque said about Jesus under that title were a lot more encouraging than the version we got at primary school. There was even a chance that you could guarantee here and now and quite easily that all would be well in the eyes of Jesus when the moment came to die. That was a big plus for me.

Then too I rediscovered Saint Thérèse of Lisieux. I say 'rediscovered' because one of the first books I read for myself as a young child was a simple life of Thérèse which happened to be on the bookshelf in the bedroom I shared at home with my brother, and I had already taken a liking to her then. We had an annual retreat for three days at the Mount, and I found Thérèse's autobiography on the school shelves, and commandeered it each year after that for the length of the annual retreat. The old 'schizophrenia', as I have called it, continued, but the weight on the side of clemency was increasing little by little. Thérèse seemed to make getting into heaven sound so much easier than the *Catechism* would have it. The retreat only lasted three days in each year; the *Catechism* we had to learn or relearn by heart *every* day of the school year. The authorities did not seem to realize that grace is a relationship – I did not realize it myself until much, much later – so that if we were made to be afraid of God as an exacting judge, we would, like the third character in Jesus' parables about the talents, end up doing little or nothing for God. The relationship would be frozen; grace would be strangled. That *Catechism*, the Penny Catechism as it was known, was and is counter-productive as an educational tool.

Other branches of learning I was introduced to at school, and which were to bear fruit later, would include all about the Five Ways of St Thomas Aquinas, in which he tries to prove the existence of God from reason alone; I especially liked the one about how there had to be an uncaused cause, or else the whole framework of creation could not stand, also the one about design in nature and science meaning there had to be a mind behind it all. Then too we learnt a bit about Church history and social teaching and what the Councils of the Church did; and in my final years at school

I was able to read bits of Plato in the original, incuding passages arguing to the reality and nature of One God. For me it was providential that I was willingly steered into Latin, Greek and Ancient History for my final three years at school, since it gave me the wherewithal in later years to read all sorts of precious documents in the original version, including of course the Gospels.

At the age of eighteen, with only a summer holiday between schooldays and noviceship, I went to Harlaxton in Lincolnshire to join the Jesuits, the Society of Jesus, the same company who had run my schooldays at Mount St Mary's and Barlborough Hall. It was not so much that the personnel at the schools were inspiring, as that the ideal they aspired to had an irresistible appeal for me. Here I would be able to find God's will all day, every day, and be helped to do God's will once found.

The first big event leading to a greater understanding of the Trinity was the Spiritual Exercises of St Ignatius Loyola. Otherwise known as 'the thirty day retreat', this is a long, silent reflection on life so far and the life God is calling one to for the future. The retreat director was also the novice director, Father George Walkerley, SJ. The way Ignatius introduces the Trinity as such is by showing the three Persons jointly deciding what to do about the sorry state of the world, namely deciding to send the Son into the world as one of us. Then for the next three weeks out of the four weeks of the retreat, the retreatant is led to contemplate one after another the scenes of the early life, public ministry, passion, death and resurrection of Jesus. What I retained from being immersed in these gospel stories was first, a much greater consciousness of the life of Jesus as a continuous whole, and then above all, a sense of myself as a follower of Jesus: Jesus out there going places; me here behind him, following. As for the Trinity sending Jesus into the world, that was a notion new to me. I already had the ideal of joining Jesus' mission to heal the world, ever since the age of six when I knew I would have to volunteer to become a priest when I grew up: that was in the early days of the Second World War, and even as a little boy I sensed that Jesus was the only one with the answer to all the hatred and bloodshed. But to think of the Trinity as the source of the call was new.

One of the priests based at Harlaxton and giving missions round the country was Father Clifford Howell, SJ. He was a pioneer working towards the renewal of the liturgy of the Church, and this was ten years before the Second Vatican Council, so his ideas were surprising to many of us. Certainly they surprised me, but they made a lot of sense. He gave us a few talks on his favourite themes, and I remember being struck by those which touched on the Trinity.

For instance, he spoke about Exposition of the Blessed Sacrament, where the consecrated bread, the body of Christ, is placed in a monstrance and left on the altar for quiet adoration. Father Howell put it to us that our adoration should be adoration of the Way, not of the Final Home. Jesus is there under the form of bread to strengthen us on our way home, but he is not the final resting place of our journey. That gave a jolt to my notion that 'Jesus is God, God is Jesus, so what's the difference anyway?' as I had accepted it since primary school. Somewhere along the line I had come to take it for granted that you did not have to look any further if only you had Jesus. Yet once Father Howell pointed it out, it became obvious that Jesus in his words and prayers kept looking further than himself.

Father Howell was also helpful in making us see what the words of the liturgy actually say. He wrote a little book about 'Mean what you pray', and gave us novices some pointers from it. For instance, it had not occurred to me, though I had followed the Mass daily for years, that nearly all the prayers are addressed to the Father, not to Jesus. The first part of the *Gloria*, all of the offertory prayers, the collect, secret prayer (now known as the prayer over the gifts, being not silent any more), the whole of the long Eucharistic Prayer and its prefaces, the *Our Father*, the *Deliver us* and the prayer after communion – all are addressed to the Father. The only prayers spoken to Jesus are the *Lord, have mercy*, the second part of the *Gloria*, the peace prayer and the *Lamb of God* (and since 1966, one might add the acclamation after the consecration). Clifford Howell was not so much emphasizing the role of the Father, as asking us to be aware which person of the Trinity we were addressing; yet to me the big discovery was how much I had been speaking to the Father without even noticing!

Even on solemn feastdays of Jesus, as Father Howell further pointed out, the prayer of the day was addressed to God the Father, through Jesus. The number of official feast day or ordinary day prayers of the Church addressed to Jesus could be counted on one hand. Even the Masses of the Holy Spirit did not address the Holy Spirit except in the hymn sequence, but prayed to the Father asking for the Spirit through Jesus Christ. Even the Mass of the Holy Trinity had as its *Collect* prayer, its main opening prayer, the following: 'O almighty and eternal God, who hast granted Thy servants to acknowledge the glory of the eternal *Trinity* in the Confession of the true faith, and to adore the *unity* in the power of Thy majesty; we beseech Thee that, by firmness in the same faith, we may be ever protected from all adversities. Through our Lord Jesus Christ Thy Son ...' The other two main prayers of that day were also addressed to the Father, through Jesus. In the whole Missal at that time, there was not a single prayer addressed to all three Persons of the Trinity at once. In making our prayers to the Father through Jesus, of course, the Missal was following the word of Jesus saying, 'And then the Father will give you anything you ask him in my name' (John 15:16); and Paul makes the same thing plain in the practice of the early Church (e.g. Ephesians 5:20). But somehow popular puzzlement had over the years and in my part of the world mingled Father and Son not just into one God, but to all intents and purposes into one Person. Father Howell distanced them one from the other in their workings in my heart, and taught me to walk with Jesus to the Father; and for this I am very grateful.

Another talk Father Howell gave us was on the shape of
the Mass, for which he used a big capital **M** for Mass as the
memory-tag. The first part of the Mass is us (down here)
talking to God (above); the second part, namely the read-
ings and the homily, is God (above) speaking to us (below);
the third part is us (at ground level) giving to God (above);
the fourth part is God (from above) giving to us (down
here). Up, down; up, down, /\/\, **M**. What chiefly intrigued
me was where the changeover came in the giving. I had
always presumed that the consecration was the high point
of the Mass, but it now seemed better to say that first we
offer our gifts, then in the consecration Jesus unites himself
with us and our gifts, and together with him, in him,
through him we are enabled to give all glory and honour to
God the Father of Jesus. All of this time the movement of
the prayer is upwards to the Father. The first part of the
Our Father was itself still part of the upward movement,
with and in Christ. Then, only then, comes the final down-
ward movement, with *Give us this day*, the *Deliver us*, the
Give us peace, the communion, the blessing and the final
mission, all of which are gifts from God. Such a simple
mnemonic, that **M**, and it gave me a whole new outlook on
the Mass as it relates to the Trinity.

As a novice I read the autobiography of Saint Ignatius of
Loyola, the founder of the Jesuits, and more than one biography of him. His most striking reference to the Trinity
comes quite early on after his conversion; in those months
he knew God was treating him as a schoolmaster treats a
little boy when he teaches him. Ignatius already had the
practice of praying daily to each of the three Persons of the
Trinity individually; then one day he noticed himself
praying a fourth prayer to the Trinity, that is to all three
Persons together, a prayer which he found in a prayer book.
He puzzled about this – how could there be four prayers to
three Persons? – without taking too much notice. Then
some days later he was given an enormous consolation from
God, which took the form of hearing three notes making
one chord. For instance, it might have been the musical

notes C, E and G which can sound separately or be played together as a perfect triad. He could hear the triad and hear the three notes within. The experience was from God, and filled Ignatius with tears of joy for hours afterwards, and gave him a special devotion to the Trinity for the rest of his life.

I appreciated that image given to Ignatius, since I was musical, and it also happened that while a novice I read a book about science and music which taught me for the first time how notes in a major or minor chord have a real physical relationship to one another, and that is why they sound right. Play the note middle C on a guitar string, and it also simultaneously sounds G and E, albeit more quietly than the leading note. The three belong together. (The E-flat note is in there too, though quieter still, to make a minor chord.)

Father George Walkerley used on occasion to give us lectures in theology, as well as the more exhortation-type talks which might or might not include theology and scripture. One time he read us selections from *Theology and Sanity* by Frank Sheed. I was particularly impressed by the image of the Trinity in that book, where they were portrayed as two Persons loving each other, and the love between them was the Holy Spirit – the Spirit belonging to both but not completely identified with either. I was strangely moved also by the way Frank Sheed described public speaking at Hyde Park Corner or elsewhere with the Catholic Evidence Guild. He said that he had only to get launched on the subject of the Trinity, and a hungry silence would descend on the audience. People loved to hear about the mystery of God; hearing it, they were like babies who have found the milk bottle or the breast with their mouths!

Two other occasions stand out in my memory relating to the Trinity and dating from my noviceship. One was the sudden impact made on me by reading the words *Jesus intravit quoddam castellum* in my Latin Bible. The real translation is 'Jesus entered a certain village', but at first glance I read it as 'Jesus entered a certain castle'. It seemed to me clear as day that at that moment Jesus entered my 'interior castle', or else was already in there and I had not known it so clearly before. The whole notion of 'Christ within me' took on a much more real meaning. Then another time it was while reading the story of Lazarus and the rich man, it became crystal clear to me that I was the rich man, and Lazarus at my gate was none other than whoever was there at the other side of the gate of my senses: whoever I saw, heard, felt at any given moment. And, that Christ was there in the other one, Christ was there in each and every Lazarus, looking for my compassion. Later, it became equally clear that I was Lazarus in need of the riches that other people could open up to me out of their compassion, but at the time it was the beautiful but slightly confusing fact that Christ was within me and Christ was also out there asking for my compassion. There was no real need to reconcile the two thoughts at that time: both were helpful in different ways. Only later did they fit into a picture of the Trinity without seeming to contradict one another.

Chapter Three

AGE 20–29

After the Noviceship came a year in London at Manresa House, Roehampton, a year called the Juniorate during which I started teacher training and brushed up my memories of the classics, rusting somewhat since schooldays. The only memory I have of that year which might relate to the Trinity is of a strange sensation I had that came of living in London for the first time. It was as if the city of God was somewhere underneath the city of London, just as the wonder of God had been underneath the wonder of the countryside in Harlaxton during the Noviceship. In some mysterious way I was already walking the streets of heaven, if I had only had eyes to see clearly. This may not seem to have much relation to the Trinity, but I will place the experience in its slot as time goes by.

Another puzzle exercised me at this time. Did God love me for my own sake, or for Jesus' sake? Not just me, but anybody: this was a question for the human race. I think I decided in the end that in loving Jesus, God was loving another Person who would be lost without that love; and that I am another person created through the Son and I would be lost without love. It was as if Jesus was saying, 'Not just me, Father, but love these others too, please, for their sake, not just for mine. Our two sakes are equally vital.' Otherwise, if we were loved only for Jesus' sake and for no other reason, we would lose our distinctness, and it would not matter if some of us got lost, so long as Jesus was all right. I may be jumping ahead in thinking this was my conclusion at the time, but I know I asked the question.

Moving on to philosophy at Heythrop College, situated in those days in the countryside in Oxfordshire, I entered a particularly difficult time of my life, but the prayers and ideas about the Trinity continued. In fact there was one huge moment of insight that came to me ... but I will come to that shortly. I had had moments of great clarity as a novice, both about the interior castle within me where Jesus had entered, and about the poor man Lazarus at the gate of my senses. In the midst of my troubles at Heythrop it was a great comfort that such a moment of vision should return, and that all was not lost.

By this time I was familiar with the famous icon by Rublev of the three young men who visited Abraham at the oak of Mamre, as related in Genesis 18:1–15. The artist depicts them as the three Persons of the Trinity. Here was a different picture from the one presented by Frank Sheed of two Persons and the Relationship between them. Here instead were three persons sitting round a table and looking very much like one another. The emphasis was on equality: three Persons equal in majesty. Instinctively I pictured the one in the middle as the First Person, but wrongly as it would turn out when I was better informed. The one in the middle seemed to dominate the picture and the action.

Philosophy was not my favourite subject ever, in fact it was the most trying subject I have ever been asked to tackle. One of the very few joys I got from it was the conviction that 'with God there are no might-have-beens', which might seem to belong more to theology than to philosophy, but it came under the heading of 'natural theology'. So far this was only a pleasing notion to hold on to, but later on after I left Heythrop it was to become a deep and lasting conviction. God starts now: there are no regrets about yesterday, only forgiveness. This would turn out to be at the very heart of the life of the Trinity.

What I have called the huge moment of insight about the Trinity happened like this. One evening I was alone in the philosophers' chapel, praying the Stations of the Cross, or the Way of the Cross. I came to the Fifth Station, which depicts Simon of Cyrene helping Jesus to carry his Cross. The clarity that came took only an instant, but will take many lines to describe. Indeed the whole experience is with me still, so deep did it go. 'Homesickness' is the single simplest way to name the key to it. I was there instead of Simon, carrying the cross of my life with Jesus and he with me. God the Father was there at the far side of the Fourteenth Station, beyond the death and Resurrection, mine and Jesus', waiting for us. We were going home. The homesickness in my heart was the Holy Spirit in my heart. Homesickness, as I knew well from being away from home in Cork at the age of five and away from home in boarding school later on, is both a yearning from home to have me back, and a yearning in me to be back where I came from and where I belong. So, God was three Persons: the Father of Jesus, yearning for Jesus and me to come home, and Jesus, longing with me to be home, and the Yearning, the Holy Spirit. In homesickness the yearning does not just proceed from one side; the yearning is not the same as the child, nor is it the same as the parents at home: my homesickness is in me but comes from me and from home. My homesickness is also there at home.

Very soon other images came to express the same clear vision. I was like a homing pigeon which had lost its homing instinct; Jesus was like a master homing pigeon who was able to lead me back and ultimately give me back my instinct for where home lies. The whole Church, the whole world, is like a vast flock of homers who have lost the way, till Jesus gives back the heart's compass. The word 'homers' reminds me that at the time I was reading Homer's *Odyssey*; its main theme, so frequent in all literature, is homesickness.

Again, the Trinity now seemed a little like two great magnets and the magnetism between them. I was like, we humans were like, a piece of metal not normally able to be magnetized, like nickel for instance. Christ by coming to live and die with us was like pure steel who mixed his steel with our nickel so that we could begin to feel the force of magnetism that flowed through him from the Father and back to the Father. We are caught up in the 'magnetism' side by side with the 'magnet' which is Christ. An odd simile, but one that helps me.

In images more human, I was like the Prodigal Son, or like any child lost and feeling orphaned; Jesus as an unlikely elder brother (that is to say, not like the one in Jesus' story) came to remind me I had a home and a Father who was still and always anxious over me. The reminder stayed with me as homesickness. Later still, I felt myself akin to the princess in Hans Andersen's *The Twelve Swans*, a favourite story from childhood. Her mother is dead, her father is weak-willed, her stepmother is a witch who hates her, her brothers are all turned into swans, and she has been abandoned in a forest by a soldier who had not the heart to kill her as he had been instructed ... then in my new version of the story Jesus stands there and says, 'Why are you crying? You have a Father: you can have mine if you want to. You have a home: you can share mine. You have a brother: see, I have come for you. Come now; we will go home together.' That last comparison I worked out later on, but the intense feeling of being lost then wanted and supported was there right from the beginning, at the Fifth Station of the Cross in the philosophers' chapel that evening.

In the third year of my studies in philosophy I suffered a breakdown. The studies were a part of what was distressing me, and the studies were the flash-point when I finally lost my reason. I was writing an essay comparing three images used by Plato to suggest the ultimate good: *the Line, the Cave, and Beauty*. Half way through the essay I decided I had discovered the secret of the universe, and I wrote and wrote and thought and thought for eight days and nights, pretty continuously, and was completely exhausted at the end but unable to stop. In the next three months I was twice in hospital; in the second hospital I was given insulin treatement, which induces a coma. In a coma one night I had the most influential dream I have ever had, the most influential single spiritual experience I have ever had. I dreamt of my final judgement, and the verdict from a totally real Jesus, just one-to-one with nobody watching, was an enormous hug of love.

At the time the embrace was just for me; as time has gone by I have realized more and more that it was for everybody, it was for me to share. Not necessarily in the form of hugs of course, but as unconditional love and total forgiveness, since I was no more deserving of being loved like that than anyone else in the world.

My father, who was a doctor, a general practitioner, was greatly upset when the psychiatrists at first diagnosed schizophrenia. But then they changed their minds, and went for what I call manic-depression or wild mood-swings, but they called bi-polar affective disorder. I find that very interesting, looking back, since I have talked about my split picture of God as love and terror as being a kind of schizophrenia, and now here in this dream in the coma the terror side of God was completely and utterly banished from that day to this. Like Julian of Norwich, I can no longer conceive of God as being angry with me. It was Jesus who hugged me and squeezed the fear out of me, but it was the work of God, no mistake.

Something else began to go from my head to my heart. It was something I had read as a novice, from one of the ancient Christian writers. He said that in order to repent, all anyone had to do was to turn round and see that God was smiling all the time. I did not have to go all the weary way back to perfection and then turn round and be pleasing to God. Just as I was, in all the mess and trouble, I should realize that God was always the same, and always loving me.

I was not sent back to finish or repeat the third year of philosophy, but instead went to teach at St John's, then the preparatory boarding school for Beaumont College in

Berkshire. At St John's the pupils, all boys in those days, ranged from seven to twelve going on thirteen. It was a pleasant but busy sixteen-hour day, seven-day week during term-time. What it taught me further about the love of the Trinity was to do with loving with no strings. Children take so much for granted, and do not usually notice the trouble that is taken over them. I suppose most teachers would consider themselves lucky if one out of ten of their pupils came back to say 'Thank you.' Jesus did not do badly, scoring one leper out of ten. Yet how quiet God is about the many good things we enjoy every day of our lives, never demanding thanks as a condition for the good things continuing. And how regularly we forget.

Next in 1961 came four years study of theology, at Milltown Park in Dublin. The first thing there I remember concerning the Trinity was a sermon I had to preach in the refectory while the brethren got on with their dinners. We all had to go through this ordeal a few times in preparation for ordination to the priesthood and the preaching that goes alongside. In some ways the practice was kinder than having to do it in church, since there was always the thought that if the brethren did not like my sermon they at least had their dinner to enjoy. I opted to give a sermon on the Trinity, quite early on in the first year. I gave the listeners the benefit of all my knowledge gained at the Fifth Station of the Cross, including homing pigeons, magnets, Prodigal Son (not the wild swans, however) and homesickness. I was delighted when among the comments about it was one I overheard from an exceedingly bright fourth year student who wondered what I was going to do for the next four years, since I seemed to know it all already! My delight was not just at the recognition, but because it gave me confidence that theology, unlike philosophy, was going to be a subject I could understand and cope with.

In fact of course there were still endless joys ahead in the way of knowing more about God. I will recall some of them in rather a random order, since I cannot now remember just where in the four years the various interesting thoughts about God came. When we were considering the originality of Jesus, it was pointed out that the Old Testament knew nothing of the Trinity, but the early Christian writers looked back over the Scriptures and wondered if there were any hints of the Trinity that should or could have been picked up. This was not just curiosity, but to find arguments in favour of such a total novelty when debating with Jewish scholars. In writing as Christians, the earliest writers always used the traditional titles of God to refer to the One they now knew as the Father of Jesus. God was God, Jesus was Son of God, and the Spirit was Spirit of God or Spirit of Jesus. Practically the only slide of titles from one to the other was in the word 'Lord'. One could almost say that Paul took that one divine title and gave it to Jesus as his own. 'Jesus Christ the Lord' or 'the Lord Jesus Christ' was the equivalent in Paul's writings of the custom other writers had of referring to Jesus as divine 'Son of God'.

In the Old Testament, then, where did they find hints of the Spirit? No great difficulty there, since the Spirit of God is mentioned so many times, from the beginning when the Spirit brooded over the waters, to the Spirit coming down on the tabernacle and the temple, and so on through the history of Israel. The difference with Jesus was that he spoke of God sending the Spirit, and people do not send themselves. Up till then 'Spirit of God' had really been an alternative way of talking about the one God the creator.

As for the Son of God, no one had quite expected a first-generation Son of God as one person walking the earth. It had been thought to refer to the whole people, or to the line of kings, or to be simply a vague metaphor, meaning a holy person, a person after God's own heart. But a one, real, divine Son who had always existed from the beginning . . .? Where was there any hint of that in the Scriptures? Where the early Christian writers, starting with St Paul, found the pre-existing Christ was at least partly in the Old Testament pictures of Wisdom.

The book The Wisdom of Solomon says 'For she is a reflection of eternal light, a spotless mirror of the working of God ... She is more beautiful than the sun, and excels every constellation of the stars. Compared with the light she is found to be superior, for it is surrounded by the night, but against wisdom evil does not prevail' (Wisdom 7:26ff. NRSV) Suchlike descriptions seemed to the early Christians to fit Jesus when thought of as the eternal Christ, even though Wisdom was always pictured as feminine in the old writings. We can see hints there in the book of Wisdom, if we choose to, of the future Christian creed, in which Jesus Christ is 'God from God, light from light, true God from true God'. Already St Paul calls Christ 'the power of God and the wisdom of God' (1 Corinthians 1:24); for Paul, Christ is the image of God (2 Corinthians 4:4), since we look at Christ to see what his Father is really like. 'He is the image of the invisible God, the firstborn of all creation' (Colossians 1:15). In Christ 'are hidden all the treasures of wisdom and knowledge' (Ibid. 2:3).

The theme of Wisdom as a foretelling of the Christ continues to be found later, as in the writings of St Justin (c.AD 100–165) and in Tertullian (c.AD 160–225). Justin is writing to try and persuade the Jew Trypho of the presence of the Trinity in the Old Testament (*Dialogue with Trypho,* ch. 61) and Tertullian is countering the view of the heretic Praxeas that there is only one Person in God. In the course of his argument he takes three chapters to insist that the Word of God is also the Wisdom of God, and is a Second Person, through whom all things were created, according to the divine plan (*Against Praxeas,* Chapters 5–7).

What really ignited my interest once and for all in theology was the Gospel of St Mark. Father Kevin Smyth, SJ who was one of our lecturers in the first year mentioned one day the suggestion of the biblical scholar Cuthbert H. Turner – that some of Mark's phraseology could be explained by its having been originally spoken by Peter, then turned into third person. Thus, Peter would have said in his preaching of the story of Jairus' daughter, *And he allowed no one to follow him except me and James and John the brother of*

James. When we came to the house of the ruler of the syna-gogue, he saw a tumult, and people weeping and wailing loudly. Turn that into third person speech, and it becomes the way Mark wrote it: *And he allowed no one to follow him except Peter and James and John the brother of James. When they came to the house of the ruler of the synagogue, he saw a tumult, and people weeping and wailing loudly.*

I decided to experiment, and turned the whole of the Gospel of Mark back into the way Peter would have told it in the first person. I used the Revised Standard Version, which seemed to be the most faithful of the versions to the original Greek. It worked like a dream.

Not only did it work like a dream, but the Gospel came alive for me as I wrote it out word by word and verse by verse. All my personal theology came out of that Gospel, as I dovetailed it in with the lectures that were running along-side each day. I wrote a long rambling book about it, which was only finished in its first version during my last year at Milltown, so I will put down some of the results, in so far as they relate to the Trinity, in the next chapter.

Chapter Four

AGE 30–40

At the age of thirty I was ordained priest, in Dublin at the end of my third year of theology. I had another year in which to finish the book on St Mark, as a part-time study and as an inspiration to the rest of the work in theology. The various themes I had discovered began to come together and make sense together. The key to much of what I saw was that moment of understanding of my place alongside Jesus in the Trinity, which I had been given back there in the chapel of the philosophers at Heythrop. I found in Mark's Gospel a theology which supported and clarified the intuitions I had received, of the unquestioning love of Jesus and of the Father which I experienced in the insulin coma, as well as in that earlier simple vision of the Trinity.

If Jesus came on earth to heal physical illness, he did not do very well. This fact had puzzled and troubled me for years. What had the stories of Jesus healing to do with me? There were a few hundred healed by his presence, and there seem to have been some instances of faith healing physical ills in every generation since. But by and large most people still get illnesses and have to go through with them. The difference Jesus made to medicine was not great, at that level. What struck me when I studied the healing stories in Mark's Gospel was that they were signs of something deeper. I knew from experience that being completely loved by Jesus, and knowing the love to be from God, made a dramatic difference to my life. To be loved now, with a complete disregard of any sins or faults of my past ... this was love with no conditions, and time-less, and revolutionary.

St Mark's Gospel tells us that Jesus brought Good News from God straight after his baptism and temptations. If we ask, 'What Good News?', the only news from God so far in the Gospel is that Jesus is the beloved Son of God, on whom God's favour rests. That was news; it was good news, that God had sent his Son to us and acknowledged him as the beloved Son. In the temptations Jesus came to grips with his vocation to share his sonship with the rest of the human race, as his beloved sisters and brothers. That was good news, indeed the best of news and completely new, for the rest of us.

This truth once believed would, I could see, free anyone from the paralysis of fear about past sins, as it had freed me from my fears. It would free anyone from feeling like a leper, inferior to those around, as it had freed me. And so on through all the stories of healing in the chapters of Mark that followed. The Good News had already set me free from anxiety about the past, free from competition with others, free from anxiety about what to do next, free from loneli-ness, free from fear of death. The Good News sets people free if they will only believe it. At long last I had a vocation within my vocation as a priest, something I had experienced and yet something I could share as coming straight from the gospel story. The sheer wonder of being God's first-genera-tion child, and the freedom and peace that followed, was something I knew I would go to the ends of the earth to share, if nobody right here would listen.

As much as anything it was the overall shape of the Gospel of Mark that taught me about the Trinity, and about the place of the Holy Spirit in the Trinity. There are sixteen chapters in the Gospel, and in all the first eight of them there is no command to do anything virtuous, except to let myself be healed, and to let myself be fed by Jesus, and to believe he comes from God. As the Holy Spirit proceeds from the Father to the Son, so it seemed the same Spirit proceeds or comes freely to each and every child of God. There are no conditions; I just need to let myself be forgiven, and then to let myself be fed and nourished into the likeness of Jesus, putting all my trust in his word. There is bread in plenty, and water in plenty, but no chalice in the first half of the Gospel.

The second half of the Gospel shows Jesus giving the right response to that unquestioning love. Jesus made it clear that we could not follow until he had died and sent us his Spirit, but now he has died, and has sent the Spirit, so now we can follow Jesus. The Spirit now goes back as always from Jesus to the Father, but also from me to the Father. The Spirit proceeds from the Son back to the Father, and from me another child of God sharing his Spirit, back to the Father.

The chalice side of things, the second half of the Gospel, braving the dangers involved in witnessing to the world one's kinship to God, the sufferings ... this second direction of the Spirit has to be prayed for before we can follow Jesus into it. As Peter and so many others have found, we cannot walk blithely into temptation and expect to triumph, if we have not prayed. The first half of the Gospel comes free: we do not have to take up the Cross and follow Jesus in order to be saved by Jesus. But the second half of the Gospel is costly, and belongs to those who wish to bring the Good News of the first half of the Gospel to the whole world.

It had been easy for me to see how the two directions of the Spirit, from Father to Son and from Son back to the Father, are there in the story of the Prodigal Son, are there in the homing pigeon image, are there in the image of the two magnets. Now here they were loud and clear in the very shape of Mark's Gospel. I could see the same pattern even there in the seed parables Mark quotes in his fourth chapter. The seed comes down from God, goes into the dark of the earth. If welcomed and given space, it grows back upwards by the power of God and becomes fruitful.

The seed, I could now see, was the word of God that says, 'You are my beloved (first-generation) child; my favour rests on you.' If I believe that with all my heart, the same word grows and takes me over completely. It comes down from above, and then grows back up.

The other Gospels, of Matthew, Luke and John, do not separate the two sides of the Spirit's work so clearly, and I was glad to have been drawn into Mark first and foremost. The Spirit like a strong wind comes to me, and, again like the wind, does not stop when it reaches a solid body. It either blows through it and makes a melody, or else it urges the solid body to go where the wind is going. The action of the Holy Spirit plays a different tune once it reaches me and has found a home: that I had already felt and known. The Spirit having gently entered me urges me to great gratitude, in return for the love that asks no questions.

Mark's Gospel was the first to be written, and does not speak so much about Father, Son, Spirit as John does in his Gospel. Nevertheless I noticed in my studies that Mark is very consistent with later tradition in the way he speaks about 'father' and 'Father'. He is the only one of the Gospel writers who gives the actual intimate word used by Jesus, '*Abba!*', when he prays in the place called Gethsemane before his arrest. Mark is the only one who has the people of Jesus' own town describe him as 'the son of Mary', without reference to any father.

When Jesus is so surrounded by people that he has no time to eat, and his family try to get to him, Jesus looks around at those who sit around him and says, 'Here are my mother and my brothers! Whoever does the will of God is my brother, and sister, and mother' (Mark 3:34f). The will of God is that we become like little children, sisters and brothers of Jesus. Already in my studies of theology I noted and pondered what it means to become mother of Jesus, and this is something to which I shall be returning; but one thing was clear, namely that nobody becomes Jesus' father except the one Father he already has.

There is a similar clarity about Mark's version when it

comes to the hundredfold promised by Jesus. 'Truly, I say to you, there is no one who has left house or brothers or sisters or mother or father or children or lands, for my sake and for the gospel, who will not receive a hundredfold now in this time, houses and brothers and sisters and mothers and children and lands, with persecutions, and in the age to come eternal life' (Mark 10:29f). A hundredfold of everything and everybody ... except fathers. There is only one Father.

Matthew reports the words of Jesus in his Gospel, 'And call no man your father on earth, for you have one Father, who is in heaven' (Matthew 23:9). This would apply not just to those who address priests or pastors as 'Father', but to every human being, since we all have someone we would normally call father. The Father of Jesus is to be seen as the first-generation Father of every single person who listens to Jesus and takes his words to heart. I was fascinated, going through the Gospel of Mark word by word in my studies and writing it out in longhand, to find these careful little distinctions in what might at first sight seem to be a rough and ready script.

Another thing that had always intrigued me was the way the Church in her liturgies clearly treats the feeding of the five thousand and the four thousand as being symbolic or prophetic of the Eucharist, so why was there no wine, but only bread and water? Mark's Chapters 5 to 8 are all about banquets, bread, water, hunger, bread of the children, one loaf, not the leaven of the Pharisees nor the leaven of Herod. But no chalice. Only when Peter has made his great acknowledgment that Jesus is the Christ does the passion of Jesus, and with it the chalice, come into the story.

I found it immensely thrilling to see the pattern of the Gospel of Mark, or at least, the pattern of the structure as it seemed to me. Many commentators on Mark's Gospel would agree about the big switch of direction after Peter's confession of faith, though they would see other shapes underlying smaller details, and would gather the overall meaning of the Gospel differently. For me, it was Part 1, healing, feeding, faith; Part 2, the Way to Jerusalem, the chalice, love. The bread of the children is for all, regardless of their qualifications other than faith in Jesus – no admission ticket to the hillside, so unlike Herod's banquet, so unlike the synagogue; the chalice on the other hand is for the strengthening of those who take up the Cross in gratitude and love and teach the Good News to the whole world. *And the two movements of the Holy Spirit correspond to the action of the bread and of the wine.* The Spirit comes with God's unquestioning love to bring food to the child of God, then invites him or her to take up the chalice out of gratitude. To me all this seemed overwhelmingly beautiful, and so, so different from the way I was taught as a child. I longed to be able to tell the whole world about it, and had high hopes for my book on St Mark's Gospel, if it should ever see the light of day. As image after image clicked into place to make a unity of what had seemed so diverse, I felt an awe such as a scientist must feel who has discovered the secret of the stars or something vast like that.

From Mark's Gospel it was clear that Jesus was Mary's son and God's Son, human and divine. The very title of the Gospel as it stands is 'The Gospel of Jesus (who is the) Christ, the Son of God', and the first half of the Gospel ends with Peter saying 'You are the Christ'; the focal point of the second half of the Gospel is the declaration of the centurion that Jesus is 'truly the Son of God'. When I added to all this the undoubted fact that the Eucharistic passages of Mark in the first half of the Gospel are all about the bread and water, the net result seemed to be that there in the first half of the Gospel we were being taught about the body of Christ, coming from Mary, his humanity. The second half of the Gospel, with its divine suffering which no human could face without the divine Spirit, belonged with the chalice. Did this mean that Mark sees in Jesus a human body with a divine life? What was the role of the water? There was water all over the place in the first eight chapters of Mark. I went researching into the early Christian writers to see what they meant by the water.

The net result of my researches was that the for the very
early Christians water in the Eucharist signifies human life.
Jesus is the divine wine who takes on our bread-and-water
humanity, in order that we bread-and-water people may
become bread-water-and-wine people like Jesus himself.
The bread 'made by hands' is for the human body, and the
water is for human life. The chalice belongs with realities
'not made with hands', is 'from heaven', is like the stone
uncut by human hands that Daniel prophesied, is of divine
origin in some sense so that it may fittingly represent the
blood of Jesus. These images come from Ignatius of
Antioch, from Justin, from Irenaeus, from Tertullian. There
is mention, for instance, of some heretics who celebrated
the Eucharist with bread and water only, considering themselves unworthy of sharing the divinity! These same images
may be found reflected already in the Gospels themselves,
notably in the story of the wedding at Cana, when the water
was changed into wine by Jesus. This was a sign, the first of
the signs, and it was a sign of Jesus' work of changing
human life into divine life. The little prayer at the offertory
in the Mass where water is poured into the wine expresses
the thought perfectly to this day: 'By the mystery of this
water and wine may we (bread-and-water people) come to
share in the divinity (wine) of Christ, who humbled himself
(wine) to become sharer in our humanity (bread and
water).'

During my studies in theology I was still struggling to
understand the redemption Jesus worked for us, and how it
worked. But here in the sweeping images of Mark were the
makings of an answer. The Gospel was in two halves; the
first half was to do with baptism as children of God and
with bread and water; the second half was to do with wine,
chalice, suffering, divinity, with doing things that mere
humanity could never reach to.

I have a fondness for images; I think in pictures. There
were at least six two-faceted images that fascinated me as I
studied Mark's Gospel, since they seemed each to have two
contradictory meanings. The images I mean are fire, water,

rock, tree, wind, and bread. Fire could destroy, or it could refine; water could drown, or it could sustain and even nourish; rock could fall on you, or it could hold you up; there was a tree doomed to destruction, and a tree of eternal life; the wind could blow contrary, or it could bowl you along; bread could be poisonous, or it could be life-giving. The key to the difference was the Holy Spirit. If I was facing God and letting the Spirit come into my heart with God's unquestioning love, then my heart would be set on fire with love in return, and with a determination to tell the world about God's love. There would still be trials and troubles to go through, including the fire of persecution, but it would bring the gold away from the dross in me, and be for my good. If on the other hand I was facing away from God and refusing the offered love and forgiveness, then the nature of love is such that I would be facing nothing but the fire of desolation.

And so it was with the other five images. The waters of baptism brought the Holy Spirit to those who welcomed God's forgiveness. The waters of the sea drowned the Legion of evil spirits who were tormenting the demoniac. The waters rose up against the disciples in the boats when they were relying on their own efforts, but subsided when they relied on Jesus. The rock represented Jesus' teaching, that we should rely on God alone as our first-generation Father. This was what Peter was destined to preach, but as long as he faced the wrong way he risked having the rock fall upon him; alternatively, he risked being dumped in the unfriendly sea like a millstone. The tree also risks being dumped in the sea when faith in God's love takes the leading place. The fig tree was unable to produce fruit at all seasons, just as the temple and its beautiful stones was unable to be found fruitful at all seasons. The tree faded away, as would the temple, but the Tree of Life, the Cross, was and is fruitful every time anyone comes to it for help and mercy. (Peter and Paul both talked about the Cross as 'the tree', which may have been a current slang way of describing an execution cross, but which none the less suited the message of the apostles very conveniently.) The wind could be contrary for those in the boat who were resisting God's way of looking at things, but would quickly carry to the shore those who relied on Jesus. Jesus' teaching was wholesome bread, free and plentiful, whereas the leaven the Pharisees and Herod added to their teaching was poison.

If we ask how it is that the same picture can give such opposing senses, perhaps the best clue lies in the parable Matthew quotes in his Gospel about the talents (there is a similar one in Luke's Gospel). The man in the story coming back from abroad is generous with those who do well, but quite harsh with the one who was a failure. This does not mean that God is generous with those who do well but harsh with the failures among us, quite clearly from Jesus' own kindly treatment of failures. It does mean that those who believe God to be generous will flourish in real terms, whereas those who picture God as being like 'a hard man, who reaps where he has not sown and gathers where he has not scattered' will stunt their own growth, because they will be too afraid of making mistakes. The nature of reality is such that if we accept God's unquestioning love we will find a deep happiness, indeed a treasure, whereas if we do not believe in that love we will find the wind against us, the stone on top of us, the tree withering, the waves engulfing us, the fire burning us. God is love, God is forgiveness. That is the truth, that is the nature of reality. If we believe reality to be anything else then we will have a distorted view of life. Nothing will satisfy us, nothing will go smoothly.

All this is true in our present life on earth; it is not saying that reality **will** at some judgement day rebound on those who do not believe in God's love (or in God as love), but that reality is **already** at work in this way. There is in fact only one direction in which the Spirit of God moves, and that is the way of love and forgiveness. Anyone who tries to move in the other direction is battling in the face of truth, and may win the odd battle but will not win the war. If we think of the Trinity alone, that direction is from the Father to the Son in unconditional love, then from the Son back to the Father equally unconditional but the motive is gratitude. If we think of God and the human race, the direction of the Spirit is from God to us in Christ with unconditional love and forgiveness, then from us in Christ back to the Father, expressed in unconditional love and forgiveness for friend and foe alike. This is the God-like fruit that God is looking for.

As it happens, I am writing this page on the feast of Saint Ignatius of Antioch, who wrote his classic letters only a generation or two after the Gospels. One of my favourite sayings from the many of his that I love is this: 'Faith is the beginning; love is the end; and the union of the two together is God.' (Ignatius *To the Ephesians* 14) In our human experience, we begin by **believing** that God is love and forgiveness; then grounded in that love we begin ourselves **to love**. The Spirit is moving us in the right direction, and we are in the same rhythm as the Trinity. (*See Diagram 1, p. 109.*)

Before I leave Mark's Gospel and the time of studies in theology, there are a couple of other themes which suggested themselves but which I did not work through at that time. I hope to return to them later in the story. One was the figure in the background in many of Jesus' parables; the other was the fact of Jesus' being cast outside the city of Jerusalem to be crucified. There is often a senior figure behind the scenes in Jesus' stories: there is the king whose son is to be married; there is the father of James and John who owns the boat and also hires other helpers, and whom they leave to follow Jesus; the farmer consults the owner of the vineyard about chopping down the tree, and they decide to be lenient; the servants are for pulling out the weeds without delay, whereas the owner of the land says to wait till the harvest. If there is to be a little child, there must be a suitable adult to see the child safely across the road. And so on.

The point about Jesus being cast outside the city is that Jerusalem was to be the bride of God, and Jesus is the seed, the Word of God. There could have been a wedding between God and Jerusalem, but the bride rejected the seed. This, however, is the seed of God, which will be fruitful wherever it falls. Hence the land outside Jerusalem becomes the bride, and the whole unrestricted earth is made fruitful. Instead of Jerusalem being the mother of all who would follow Christ, there is a new Jerusalem which does not depend on Jewish territory or practices. The old Jerusalem is part of the whole earth, so has the same share as anywhere else in God's unquestioning love, but she is no longer the exclusive channel.

When I left Dublin and the studies in theology, I went to North Wales for what we call Tertianship, a kind of third year of Noviceship. Then I was posted to Loyola Hall near Liverpool as a retreat giver for a year, did a year in Belgium at Lumen Vitae to study catechetics (the art of sharing religion), then another year at Loyola Hall, followed by a year in Scotland setting up a catechetical centre in Glasgow, a year teaching as acting head of the Department of Religious Education in a Secondary Modern school in Widnes, Cheshire, and finally with a sigh of relief settled down as a member of the Christian Education Centre team in Liverpool, as an adviser to the Catholic religious teachers of the archdiocese. There was a lot of experience packed into those years between theology in Dublin and starting at the education centre in Liverpool, but at last I had time and opportunity to piece thoughts together again, in the company of experienced catechists. Trying to present the truths simply and effectively to teachers meant finally beginning to understand many new truths myself.

Chapter Five

AGE 40–50

I was in fact only thirty-seven years old when I was invited to join the team of the Christian Education Centre, but it did take at least three years for some of my notions about theology to reshape themselves. I had this absolute conviction that God through Jesus had completely forgiven me there at the time of my breakdown when I was twenty-four, and along with that there was the conviction that the forgiveness was eternal, for every day in the future as well as for every day in the past. The Jesus I would meet when I die will be the same as the Jesus who waited for me in my dream. For some years I had mainly applied this knowledge of forgiveness to myself. Now it was becoming clearer and clearer that the invitation was there from God to tell any and all of God's children the same thing, if I could only reach them and if they would only listen. It was no mean task to square that with the kind of teaching which children like myself (my childhood home in Wigan belonged in the Liverpool Archdiocese) had received a generation before. In fact it could not be squared at all: teaching at child level had moved too far away from the Gospel. Many teachers welcomed a new way of looking at life in the light of the Gospels; many did not, because it implied they had been teaching less than the truth for years.

I mentioned in the last chapter that I found the idea of

redemption difficult to understand. This being so, it was obviously difficult to help school teachers to understand it as well. Some of my fellow teachers in the school in Widnes had a very gloomy and tortured version of why Jesus had to die, giving the poor teenage children the impression that they personally had nailed Jesus to the Cross, and that they should grieve over every drop of blood on that account. The students listened politely enough, but were by no means convinced. St Ignatius in the Spiritual Exercises had spoken of how the three divine Persons gazed upon the earth in its distress and decided in their eternity that the Second Person should become human to save the human race. Save us from what? And how? And why a cross? And what had the Jesus on the Cross to do with me?

The understanding that grew, and that fitted perfectly with what I had experienced of God's love and forgiveness in my own life was like this: what the three Persons of the Trinity wanted to make clear to the world was that God is love, and God is forgiveness. This was the Good News that was neither heard nor understood in the time before Christ. Using our own human understanding of parental love and family love at its best as the model, Jesus was to share with the rest of us his relationship with his Father. In a good family every child is as precious as the others. In a good family the parents love the children whether they do well or whether they do badly. Such was the nature of God's love for us humans that Jesus preached.

Jesus made enemies, because the religion he grew up in was exclusive, whereas Jesus preached a religion that reached everyone, good, bad or indifferent. The local religious leaders were supported by the Romans; Jesus was attracting crowds thousands deep, arousing the suspicions of the Roman conquerers. Jesus did not subscribe to the zealous patriotic movement, which would have welcomed his support and his popularity as a means of driving out the Romans. He could have changed his message to suit the local religion and its leaders, or to suit the Romans or to suit the zealots, but he remained true to the mission given him by the Trinity. So he was removed from the scene by his enemies, but replaced on the scene by his Father in such a way that his enemies could no longer touch him.

Jesus did not die on a cross because his Father wanted him to die on a cross. Jesus died rather than deny the truth he came to tell us, that we are each first-generation children of God his Father, loved and forgiven. As for my own salvation, I could put it this way: if his enemies had offered Jesus a deal, that he could continue to live so long as he condemned me, Gerald Anthony O'Mahony, Jesus would have died first. And any one of us who lives on this earth can say the same. In that very real sense, Jesus died for me; and he was my only chance to know that the Truth loves and forgives me without conditions.

A big help to me was a book by Peter de Rosa entitled *God our Saviour*, which took all my confidence back to where it had started in my life: to 'Holy God'. God the First Person wanted me safe; God wanted me to know he loved me with an everlasting love; God knew I was always weak and often sinful and did not love me less on that account. Jesus was the one who died so that I would know myself loved and forgiven by the One who is truth. God's love is what saves me, and it was Jesus who delivered it to me, down through the ages by means of his disciples and their successors. I do not have to save my soul: God alone is the one to save my soul.

Little by little I was rewriting my understanding of Christian doctrine, starting from the foundation stone of '*Abba! Father!*' If God was really like the father of the Prodigal Son, and if Jesus still felt the same about sinners as he did in his last will and testament on the Cross, then much of what I had learned as a child would have to be thrown into the air and allowed to come down again in a new formation. For instance, what about the sacraments of baptism and confirmation?

My studies in Mark's Gospel had convinced me that the baptism of Jesus is the model for our baptism, and that the transfiguration of Jesus is the model for our sacrament of

confirmation. Baptism sows the seed of God's unconditional love in our hearts. In fact it celebrates something that
is already true, since God does not start loving us only when
we are baptized. But the celebration brings home the
wonderful truth. The heavens are split open, the Spirit
comes down with an olive branch, the Father claims his
child as a young sister or brother of Jesus. The child is then
welcome to eat the bread of the children at the Father's
table. In the sacrament of confirmation, on the other hand,
we celebrate the call of God to respond with Jesus in loving
God back without conditions. The call or invitation is
always secondary: God never calls without first loving the
one he calls. In the sacrament of confirmation there is a
mountain to scale, the Spirit is more mysterious and cloud-
like, and the voice of God is saying 'This is my beloved
child; listen to her, listen to him'. We are called to witness
to who we are, God's own children, no matter what it costs,
no matter how painful the chalice. In other words, baptism
corresponds to the first half of Mark's Gospel, and confirmation corresponds to the second half. Because of the
direction in which the Spirit moves, no one can be
confirmed before they are baptized. Also, baptism is free
and makes no conditions, whereas confirmation is costly.

I know this understanding of baptism as completely
unconditional is not fashionable, even after Vatican II.
Among catechists at least, there is still a desire to see
baptism as some kind of commitment to the Cross of Jesus,
thus blurring the distinction between the first half and the
second half of Mark's Gospel. To me that distinction
matters enormously, because it comes from the very nature
of the Trinity. God the Father of Jesus loves the Son with no
conditions, and the Spirit seals that love. The Son then and
in gratitude loves God the Father back with no conditions,
and the Spirit seals **that** love. Baptism echoes the first movement of the Spirit; our confirmation echoes the second
movement of the Spirit. Unless we are to know ourselves
loved with no conditions, no strings, no 'provided that', no
'but only if', then we will never find the power of the Spirit

of Jesus to love unconditionally like that in return. In the Roman Catholic Church the sacrament of confirmation has always been regarded as an optional sacrament. This matches what I say about the second half of the Gospel being voluntary: the more I see myself loved freely by God, the more I will **want** to love God back.

Another sacrament of the Catholic Church, which seemed to me in the form in which it was practised to be contrary to the central doctrine of '*Abba!*' was the sacrament of reconciliation. I had been taught that at times the sacrament was absolutely necessary if my sins were to be forgiven, and that I could be cast into hell if I did not get to confession in time. Let nobody say 'Oh, nonsense!', because as I said before I was a clever child and I have a very good memory. This version of affairs made it obviously easier for anyone who was not a Catholic to have their sins forgiven, since they had only to ask for forgiveness and they would get it, whereas I would have to go through the ordeal of telling my sins and getting the story right. The fact of the matter is, I now saw, that God has forgiven me from eternity into eternity, and all I have to do is want to be forgiven. The sacrament of reconciliation is a way of celebrating the permanent forgiveness, and of bringing it home to myself in a tangible form.

The first book I ever wrote was about forgiveness. I called it *Seventy Times Seven*, for the number of times in the day we must forgive one another. When it was reprinted, it bore the title *The Gift of Forgiveness*. It was short and simple, being really a compilation of the talks, homilies and sermons I had given on the subject since my ordination. It dealt quite neatly with the angry passages in the Gospels, where Jesus condemns the Pharisees and scribes and lawyers: it had occurred to me that the only people Jesus ever condemned were those who condemned others; the only people Jesus excluded from his kingdom were those who wanted to exclude others. If Jesus is for total forgiveness, then obviously he cannot tolerate intolerance. It was as simple as that.

During my time at Loyola Hall I had read a good biography of Martin Luther which was on the library shelves. I was both delighted and slightly alarmed by it. I was delighted to have found someone in history who saw this matter of forgiveness as clearly as I had come to see it. I was slightly alarmed because it was slightly alarming for a Roman Catholic to find the most sympathetic ear in one who was usually regarded as a major heretic. In fact there was no need for alarm, since Luther's starting point, justification by faith, is something that can be agreed by a Catholic without necessarily going on to sweep away as many aspects of Catholicism as Luther subsequently did. What justifies me is my belief and trust that God loves me without conditions; in the light of that belief I positively want to do all I can to thank such a good Creator and God.

I am giving the impression that Martin Luther was the only person I found to agree with me on this matter. There had been times when it felt like that. Looking back on my year of Tertianship, when I was only thirty or thirty-one years old, there were two things above all stayed with me. One was negative, the other most positive. The negative was this: one time the priest-in-charge, the Tertian Instructor as he was called at the time, told me, 'Your God is too soft'. I was very angry to hear him say that, though I did not tell him so. I had been through hell in two nervous breakdowns, of which there were more to come, and God had been anything but too soft with me. I was to go through a different kind of hell in the year in Scotland, where my 'too soft God' was not appreciated and I was forced out of the country by the diocesan authorities. Kind and wonderful as Father Paul Kennedy (the Tertian Instructor) was in so many ways, he seemed quite incapable of understanding what I was on about. Little wonder that I took quite some time to find the confidence to say plainly what I could see so plainly. It was an enormous relief to find myself at the age of thirty-seven onwards, in the Christian Education Centre working with priests and sisters who already understood and taught my kind of theology.

The one most positive thought to come when I reflected on the time of Tertianship was again to do with the Trinity. Looking back, and comparing the experience of the thirty-day Spiritual Exercises as a novice with the experience of the same thirty-day Exercises in the Tertianship, I noticed something strange and rather wonderful. As a novice at the age of eighteen I had gone through the life of Jesus picturing myself into the scenes of the gospel stories as an observer and follower. Jesus was doing the work, I was following along behind, learning the ropes, watching him in action. When it came to the same stage of the Exercises as a Tertian, I had just naturally found myself looking out through the eyes of Jesus, particularly in the death of Jesus. No longer was I down there looking up at Jesus dying for me; I was up on the Cross, one with Jesus, on the same Cross, with the same body.

This took some time to dawn on me, which is why I did not mention it in the previous chapter of this present account. From this change of focus I learnt something new, that when we have been following Jesus for some time and then seem to lose the feeling of his company, the reason may not be our hearts going cool, but that we have become identified with Jesus who now looks out through our own eyes. Small wonder, then, if we can no longer see him. But after all, we have probably prayed many times to Jesus to take our eyes, our hands, our ears, our feet, our hearts, and use them as his own. Why then be surprised if he does that? Yet we may miss the 'otherness' of following someone 'out there' which we had before. From this change of experience came eventually the sense that being loved without strings by God is warm and comforting, whereas loving God back without strings means giving warmth to others, and feeling cold.

Reassurance comes from the words of Mark's Gospel (and Luke's). When I am baptized, it is as if the voice from heaven says to me personally 'You are my beloved son' or 'You are my beloved daughter'. When I am confirmed and called to act like a child of God as well as simply to believe

I am one, the voice from heaven says to the world at large, 'This is my beloved son' or 'This is my beloved daughter' then adds, 'Listen to him' or 'Listen to her'. Distinctly chillier than the first word from heaven, but the reassurance is in the word 'beloved'. I am still and always 'the beloved', even when I am invited in this way to speak up for who I am. When Jesus takes me over to make a disciple of me, he has in fact come infinitely closer, not gone away. The second direction of the Spirit takes up and transforms what was there before: the lamb has become a shepherd, without ceasing to be a lamb. 'I know I am a sinner, but God loves me as his beloved child. I proclaim this same glory to be open to anyone at all.'

Another pattern was beginning to form in my mind, or rather I was beginning to see another pattern already there in the Gospels. Take that image I just mentioned, of the lamb who becomes a shepherd. Jesus who came from somewhere outside was the Lamb of God from the start of his public ministry, and quickly became a good shepherd. The same language can be used of Christians who follow the shepherd. To begin with, we are lost sheep or lambs, then sheep or lambs found, then the sheep or lambs are called to be shepherds. Similarly, Jesus insists on being 'caught' in the net of God's love in the waters of baptism, then he fishes for Peter and Andrew and James and John. The four fishers are first of all like so many fish caught in Jesus' net, then they are called to be fishers of people. Lambs do not normally become shepherds; fish do not normally become fishers. The second half of the Gospel needs an extra marvel on top of the first wonder of being loved with no conditions. We are mirrors, as Jesus was a mirror; we can only show what has been shown to us. My shaky sand foundation can be turned into rock. My field has to be sown by God but then I can become fruitful. I have to be shown the Way before I can show others, and this will often mean my first having to be rescued from robbers along the way. These thoughts and images were working inside me over these years, but were for the most part not yet formulated enough to present to teachers. If the occasion arose, I could use one or other for a particular situation.

One aspect of dogma which did come up quite frequently was original sin. For some reason I cannot now remember, many Catholic teachers had decided that the doctrine of original sin was under threat, and they wanted to hang on to it. The reason may have been the gradual dawning that the story of Adam and Eve was not a historical event but an artistic way of describing a real problem. For the reshaping of theology which I was doing for myself and the teachers I found the heart of the problem in 'lack of trust'. Even in Adam and Eve terms the story could be understood that way: God gives a million blessings, and the pair of humans do not trust God because they have not been given number one million and one. More theologically, lack of trust is the direct opposite of the Spirit that cries out *'Abba! Father!'*, and *'Abba'* is the one word above others that sums up Jesus' message. (I had been reading *The Central Message of the New Testament* by Joachim Jeremias, which reassured me on this point at the time.) So it seemed only right that Jesus the second Adam should utterly contradict the fault of the first Adam. And indeed we are still as a human race most unwilling to trust that God loves us with no conditions. The movement of the Spirit from Father to Son, accepted, then returned to the Father from the Son is fixed: it cannot go into reverse. Lack of trust is simply resistance to the movement of the Spirit, and is the reason why so many things in this life go wrong that need not have gone wrong.

I wrote above that I was throwing the whole of my childhood theology into the air to let it come down again in a different shape. Before I left the Christian Education Centre I not only had revised the junior school syllabus for eight–eleven-year-olds, but had written and published a simple adult catechism called *Abba! Father!* which looked at the whole of Catholic theology from the starting point of God's unconditional love. Even fairly knotty doctrines like the Immaculate Conception of Mary fitted in quite neatly: if Jesus was someone who completely and always trusted God as his loving and beloved Father, then Jesus' own mother must have been a totally trusting person, by the gift of God, unlike our original mother Eve as depicted in the book of Genesis.

In that same book I wrote also about the Eucharist of course, and was beginning to be more confident in linking the material bread, water and wine with the symbolic meaning of each even before the words of consecration in the Mass. Father Clifford Howell had shown the way, in his talks to us novices, noting how the priest by the words of Christ separates the body from the blood (and the water). The only time the body of Christ was separate was when his body was on the Cross or in the tomb, and his blood and the water were on the ground or on the lance of the soldier. Here at least was one way in which I did not go along with Martin Luther, who for irrelevant reasons (he thought the water in the Eucharist stood for 'our human efforts in support of Christ') discontinued the adding of the drop of water in the Eucharist. The Lutheran Church to this day uses only bread and wine, thus unconsciously making out Jesus to be a human body with divine life but no purely human life. Later on it has become clear to me that the Resurrection is also represented there, in what follows at the Eucharist: a small particle of the consecrated bread is dropped into the chalice before Communion takes place, reuniting body, human life and divine life as happened at the first Easter. Then the presiding priest receives both the bread and the mingled wine of the Eucharist, after which those present are able to do the same, portraying the Resurrection in their own selves.

After ten years in the Christian Education Centre I was invited to become Novice Master (now entitled Novice Director) for the British Jesuit Province. From my point of view and the point of view of many others this was a sad story, since after a year of preparation I took over and lasted only two months before having a serious nervous breakdown. I am still not wholly sure what caused it. Most likely I had relaxed my guard, forgotten that I still and always had a 'bi-polar affective disorder' and let the prospect and the experience of being Superior of the house and Novice Director go to my head. Anyway, for the next three years or more I was in a certain amount of turmoil, and there are no clear reflections to report. In September 1983 I found myself back at Loyola Hall, where I have been ever since, and as the dust began to settle in my mind I began to be able to put thoughts together once more, including those that had been born out of the turmoil.

Chapter Six

AGE 50–55

I was forty-eight when this second round of breakdowns overtook me. Much later on it became clear to me that in the process of breaking down and slowly breaking through to normal life again, I had learnt something very significant about my relations with the Trinity. At the time it was just a case of riding the storm and waiting for a sense of balance to return. In one of the places I went to convalesce, my cousin Marie O'Mahony suggested that I get out my pen and start writing again, since writing had meant so much to me. From this meeting I got the impetus to get going with another book, which was published three years later. The book on St Mark was almost ready but stalled, and I had not the heart to risk failure with it again. So I took from it the themes relating to the chalice and treated them as a book on their own: *The Cup that I Drink*. Writing it gave me the opportunity to reflect deeply and at length about the place of suffering in the life of a Christian, and indeed in the life of anybody at all. The only part of this book on the chalice I want to refer to here and now is what concerns the bread, the water and the wine at the Eucharist, since this had to do with the Trinity and the Incarnation in a way that was 'out there' and such as I could cope with even at the time.

My reader will remember that in researching the early

Christian writers I had found a consistent pattern which related bread to the human body 'made with hands', water to 'human life' and wine to 'gift from heaven' or '**not** made by human hands'. By 'human life' I mean simply the difference between a body alive and a body dead, so that it includes movement, thoughts, affections, desires and so on. Jesus came to us with a purely divine life and took on our human life in a human body. His wine was united with our bread and water. In his death and Resurrection Jesus embraced our life to the bitter end and beyond, but his divinity could not be quenched, and his divinity brought his body and human life through to resurrection. These three images, the bread, the water and the wine, correspond exactly to what St Paul calls 'body, soul and Spirit'. Body and soul taken on their own constitute 'the flesh', namely bread-and-water human nature subject to temptation. Hence 'the Word' (of the One who calls God '*Abba!*') was made flesh: the wine was united with the bread and water.

What is comes to is this: the divine wine gives another dimension to us bread-and-water humans, namely the power to call God '*Abba! Father!*' There is something in us that is able to take fire from his fire, take breath from his breath. This is as it were the magnetism which enables us to cling to Jesus. Jesus takes on our bread and water, but gives us his wine, his living, breathing relationship with God as his *Abba*, his Father. This was a new thing in human history, that we should be able to think of each one of ourselves as first-generation children of God the Creator, rather than as some kind of pets in God's menagerie, fondly called 'children' in some merely patronizing sort of way (to put it crudely but forcibly).

When we link this with St Paul's assertion that it is the Spirit who makes us cry out '*Abba! Father!*', we then have the Spirit as our Advocate, there in the wine within us. Wine intoxicates, wine has mystery. As purely human beings with a human life and nothing more – bread-and-water people – we would come up on trial before God for our sins and have no rescue. But when the wine in us, the divine wine, empowers us to cry out *'Abba! Father!'*, God cannot resist the urge to forgive us, his very own children. I am no longer crying out 'Lord! Lord! See what a good servant I have been', but 'Have pity on me, your very own child, even though I lived so badly!' There never was a simpler or more effective defence lawyer than the Spirit of Jesus. This too would explain why Paul writes about our being 'one body, one Spirit' with Christ, and why he writes about our all drinking the same Spirit. The chalice at the Eucharist contains the consecrated wine-with-water, the blood of Christ, his divine and human life, given to us to share. The reality is within our hearts, but the sacrament nourishes the reality within, and puts into pictures what is happening within.

So I am not saying that only those who receive the chalice at the Eucharist are able to call God their own Father; but those signs chosen by Jesus, the bread, the water and the wine prepared for the Eucharistic Prayer which is to follow, tell their own story even before the words of consecration are spoken: 'By the mystery of this water and wine, may we come to share in the divinity of Christ, who humbled himself to share in our humanity.'

Writing about *The Cup that I Drink* gave me confidence to try another rewrite of the book on St Mark. I tried again to find a publisher for it, and got nowhere. So I started to write my own life story. This was something I had always wanted to do, but what inspired me in the end was a combination of two things: I read *Interior Castle Explored*, by Ruth Burrows, and I climbed the Mediterranean Steps in Gibraltar during a holiday there. The shape the story of my life took slipped easily into the story of a day's climbing up those steps, and it also fell naturally into seven stages, which seemed to match the seven 'mansions', or seven 'suites of rooms' in St Teresa of Avila's *The Interior Castle*.

The seven stages went like this. There was the initial fascination with God (and with climbing the steps as a project); there was the start of the climb (commitment to God); there was major disappointment of losing my sense of direction (breakdown); all was forgiven (the way up was clear again); there was growth in confidence (climbing steadily); there was last-hour crisis (more breakdown); and there was serenity (coming down the other side and home). So I wrote the book and it eventually found a publisher. The publisher's freelance agent at the time, Robert Kelly, took the book on Mark as well.

At first I felt shy of picturing myself as being in 'the seventh mansion', which sounded rather grand. On the other hand, if someone is going to write with any authority about the seventh mansion, they have to have been there. So in the faith story book, which I called *The Other Side of the Mountain,* I disguised the claim in three ways: first, I simply numbered the sections of the story 1 to 7 and did not say why; next, I pointed out clearly that lots of people (indeed everyone eventually) must go through as far as the the seventh stage on the way to full union with God; we all have to see eye to eye with God one day. The third disguise was in the title of the book, which comes from an old song the Boy Scouts used to sing, about 'the bear went over the mountain, to see what he could see ... and what do you think he saw? The other side of the mountain!' No great histrionics at reaching the summit. Once there, you go down home with great relief. In these and like ways I encourage other people since then, to look again at the great classic books of spirituality. If the end product of spirituality is so rarified that no one can understand it, who then are the great writers writing for?

The main point about the title of my story was that in some strange way life was now more about controlling than about striving. Climbing a hill or a mountain there is striving, to get to the top. Coming down the other side, there are less difficulties, and they are of a different kind. The muscles used for climbing up are different from the muscles used for coming down at a measured pace, without toppling down head over heels.

In my friendship with God I found myself talking now with God the Father, with 'Holy God' my old original friend, rather than with Jesus as Joan Higham had taught me so long ago. It felt permanently as if the father of the Prodigal Son had seen me his son appear over the top of the mountain searching for home, and had run to meet me. I seemed once again to have lost contact with Jesus, and I presumed that my elder brother, having toiled all the way uphill with me, must now have gone down ahead to prepare the supper, and left me to walk home at my own pace with my Father. This was a third turning point in my finding 'Holy God' again. The first had been following after Jesus as the way to go; the second had been finding Jesus one with myself, looking out through my eyes; the third now was to be one with the Father again, but still a long way off home.

Where the seven mansions of Theresa relate to this experience of three stages became clearer to me when I made a diagram of the interior castle progress: there was a big chasm after the third mansion, and another after the sixth mansion. (*See Diagram 2, p.110.*) Could it be that the jump from following in the footsteps of Jesus to a closer union with Jesus is none other than the moment when the Good News finally dawns on the seeker? This would be the chasm Theresa puts after the third mansion and before the fourth. And could it be that the jump from 'being one with Jesus' to 'being met by the Father' is the same as the jump from thinking I was already in charge of my destiny to recognizing I am still a creature? This would be the chasm that Theresa puts between the sixth and seventh mansions.

During the first three of Theresa's seven stages, I am learning one lesson, that I am not rubbish, I am God's child: God loves me even though I am a sinner. I am a failure through my own fault and weakness, yet God still loves me with an unshakeable love. During the fourth, fifth and sixth of Theresa's seven stages I am learning the other vital lesson, that God loves me just the same even though I am suffering through no obvious fault of my own. Just so did St Peter have to learn the hard way, that life can go desperately wrong even for those who know and accept the Good

News of God's unshakeable love. He thought that once he had his Messiah and a totally loving God, there would be no such horror as a crucifixion to come. And so we also can get above ourselves when we are aware of God's everlasting love, and we can forget that we are not God.

For myself I would see the two chasms I speak of as coinciding with my two main breakdown times. Quite recently a psychiatrist reviewing my life story and my medical records reckoned that I really had two breakdowns, not five as I put in the story. There was one at the age of twenty-four, and a relapse; and there was one at the age of forty-eight, with two relapses. I would put those two breakdowns as the two jumps across the two chasms. I always was a bit of a dramatist, so maybe I made a big drama out of transitions that most people make quite quietly and without fuss. Certain it is that I came out of the first at age twenty-four with an absolute conviction of God's everlasting love and forgiveness; and certain it is that at the age of forty-eight I walked right into a test I was not equipped for. Peter thought he would cope with being in the courtyard where Jesus was taken after the arrest; I thought I could cope with being Director of Novices.

Round about this time, when *The Other Side of the Mountain* was published, and *Praying St Mark's Gospel* along with it, another vital key came into my possession, so very quietly this time, that I cannot remember when it happened. I mean the obvious but little observed fact that Matthew's version of the Lord's Prayer starts 'Our Father', whereas Luke's starts 'Father'. For Luke there is no 'Our', no 'Thy will be done' and no 'Deliver us from evil'. I read in the same book, *The Central Message of the New Testament* already referred to, that Luke's version is almost certain to be the one Jesus taught as his master prayer, and that the disciples in Matthew's circle made the three additions. They would have reasoned, 'We each call God "Father", so therefore together we call God "Our Father"; Jesus prayed most earnestly in the Garden of Gethsemani, "Thy will be done", too late then for him to put that prayer

into his main prayer, but not too late for disciples to hear
and imitate; he prayed that we be not put to the test, but
what about when we have been put to the test and have
failed? Surely we pray then "Deliver us from the evil we
have walked into"?' That makes sense: that Jesus himself
at some distance from his sufferings taught the simpler
version given by Luke, and the three extra petitions were
added later as a result of reflection and experience. The
alternative is unthinkable, that Luke's circle of disciples
would have dropped three of the Lord's petitions on their
own authority.

What it comes to is this, that in all likelihood Jesus taught
us to pray *Abba*, 'My Father', my very own personal first-
generation Father. In my own life I have always felt a bit
different; I did and said surprising things as a child and as
a schoolboy, like playing the *encore* before the main piece
as a solo pianist at the school prizegiving, to warm my
hands because the piece printed on the programme was
tricky. Not many people have survived so many breakdowns and written books about it. I have to cut corners and
go my own way, time and again, because I see things differently. Hence I grew up very unsure that I could keep up
with Church regulations, Jesuit regulations, and even moral
obligations. There was a very real risk that I would never be
able to say 'Our Father' with complete confidence that I
was keeping up with the rest of the 'us' implied by the word
'Our'. For me it was and is a huge consolation that the one-
to-one personal relationship comes first in Jesus' teaching,
and the Church only second. For the moment the consolation was simply there. In time I would develop it as a theme
on loneliness and how the one-to-one relationhip with God
is the cure for loneliness and is itself the impetus of the
Church, and I will return to that theme later in its place.

Somewhere around this time I read a better guide to the
Rublev icon of the Trinity I mentioned earlier on. The
figure in the middle, it turned out, was the Second Person,
wearing the purple tunic and blue cloak usual for the Christ
figure in icons, with the striped stole over his right shoulder

and displaying two fingers for his humanity and his divinity. The Father and the Spirit have given the Christ centre
stage. The figure on the viewer's left was the Father, golden
in glory. The one on the right in blue and green was the
Spirit. Behind the Father was a house, the house of God or
the home of Abraham. Behind the Son was the tree, the tree
of the Cross or the oak of Mamre. Behind the Spirit was the
rock the water came from. They each had wings, as the
angels from the Genesis story; they each had a pilgrim's
staff (it was pleasant to think of God as still travelling, not
stationary); they each looked young, of about the same age
(and it was good to think of God as being forever young).

The give-away to the picture's being from the Eastern
Church is in the eyes of the three Persons: where are they
looking? The line starts with the Father, who looks across
at the Spirit, as if to ask the Spirit please to offer the chalice
on the table to the Son. The Spirit looks at the chalice, and
is about to move it over to the Son. The Son stretches out
his right hand, first and second fingers extended, to take the
cup, but he is looking lovingly at the Father. In terms of
action, the Spirit comes between the Father and the Son, but
not between the Son and the Father, or rather not emanat-
ing from the Son when he looks back to the Father. The
Spirit proceeds from the Father, but not from the Son. And
this is the main historical difference between the theology of
the Church of the East and the Church of the West.

This aspect of the Rublev icon would not do for me at all.
I could go along with the equality of dignity, with the
images of house, tree and rock, with the ever-young appear-
ance of the figures and their pilgrim staffs, with the love in
their eyes and with the conference resulting in the chalice
being taken by the Son. But, for my part, the Spirit would
have to be in the centre, conveying the love and request in
one direction and the love-in-return and the acceptance in
the other direction. The Spirit could not, in the picture,
direct eyes in both directions at once, but would still have
two ears, one to listen to the Father and then with his
mouth to speak the message to the Son, and one to listen to

the Son's reply then to turn and speak the reply to the Father. I was beginning to have a sense of this 'Spirit proceeding from the Father **and** from the Son' as being at the centre of so many things: the story of the Prodigal Son, the Shepherd and the lamb, the light and the mirror, baptism and confirmation, the baptism of Jesus and his transfiguration ... so many key places in the Christian tradition had two sides to them.

In my study of the Gospels in the original Greek, during the time of theology, one word among many that began to mean a lot to me was *kolpos*. This is a word meaning 'bay', 'the part of the seashore between two headlands', but then also 'lap' of the human body, meaning the bay between the headland of the head and the jutting of the knees when a person is sitting down or reclining. Hence 'the beloved disciple' at the final supper of Jesus' life was reclining next to Jesus. The text says he was reclining in the bay of Jesus (John 13:23). Next comes the realization that the word *kolpos* has been used before. In the Prologue of John's Gospel it is said that the only-begotten Son who is 'into the bay of the Father', he has made the Father known. The Jerusalem Bible translation is 'who is nearest to the Father's heart' (John 1:18). Accordingly, 'the beloved disciple' is being pictured as 'nearest to the heart of Jesus'. As Jesus is nearest to the Father's heart, so the beloved disciple is nearest to Jesus' heart; as the beloved disciple is nearest to Jesus' heart, and so too the reader or hearer of the Gospel is nearest to the disciple's heart. The Father is the Great Shepherd, and the Son is the Lamb of God; the Lamb becomes the Good Shepherd, and the beloved disciple is the lamb. The disciple in turn becomes a shepherd, and **his** disciple becomes the lamb. 'As the Father loved me, so have I loved you; as I have loved you, so love one another.' In the same way and with the same kind of love that you have experienced, so love one another. The Father is the Light, and Jesus is the true reflection of the one Light; the mirror which is Jesus enlightens in turn the mirror which is the beloved disciple, and then that mirror shines on another mirror, which shines on another mirror, and so on forever. One Light always, but many mirrors. The Light has to be unquestioning love, love with no strings, unconditional love, and it starts with the First Person.

There is a difference in the wording in the two places in John where *kolpos* appears. The only-begotten Son (or, as some manuscripts have it, 'the only begotten God') is **into** the lap (bosom, heart) of the Father, whereas the beloved disciple and all who follow are simply **in** the lap (bosom, heart) of Jesus. I have tried to illustrate the difference in my *Diagram 3* (*see p. 111*), indicating that the Second Person of the Trinity has two ways to face, one within the Trinity and the other when reaching out into the human race, generation after generation. Within the Trinity, the Father loves the Son, the Son in return loves the Father, and love is fulfilled. But then, freely, the love that asks no questions reaches out into creation, and teaches some from each generation, any who will listen, about love with no demands.

In the reordering of the words of the Roman Catholic liturgy after the Second Vatican Council, a slight but unhelpful change was made in the English versions, to the ending of the main prayers of the Mass. The prayers in Latin have for centuries, as we have seen, been addressed to the Father and always end with *per Christum Dominum nostrum*, or some similar wording: 'through Christ our Lord.' In the 'Englishing' of the prayers it was thought that the sentences of the Collect prayers were often too long, and they were broken up into smaller sentences. Then to avoid lengthening them all over again by adding on the 'through Jesus Christ our Lord', or even more so by 'through Jesus Christ our Lord who lives and reigns with you in the unity of the Holy Spirit for ever and ever', the words about Christ were made into a separate sentence: 'We ask this through Christ our Lord', or else sometimes, 'Grant this through Christ our Lord', or, 'Grant this in the name of Jesus the Lord'. This was maybe helpful to the understanding of the prayers in the vernacular, but was not helpful to the understanding of the place of the Lord Jesus Christ in the Trinity. Jesus Christ is the mediator; he receives the Holy Spirit and he sends the Holy Spirit. He receives from the Father and he sends to us as well as back to his Father. Our prayers ascend to the Father through Christ and the gifts from God come down to us in Jesus' name. The new English form of the prayers only looks in one direction at a time. Either we are going upwards to God through Christ, or God is coming down to us through Christ. Never both ways at once. With the Latin *per Christum Dominum nostrum,* it was clear that the traffic between heaven and earth went both ways through Jesus all the time.

Lastly in this chapter I would like to give a couple of images to suggest what the love of Jesus for his Father in the Trinity looks like, and the love of Jesus for us **and** at the same time for his Father looks like. I mentioned many pages ago the image of the Trinity given by Frank Sheed, of two people and the love between them. To my mind the most pefect example of that is to be found in the painting by Rembrandt and the drawing by the same artist, of the return of the Prodigal Son. The father in both pictures clasps the son to his bosom, and is perfectly oblivious of the ragged and wretched state of the boy. My reader may ask, but is not Christ perfect, surely he has nothing to regret? How can such a scruffy character represent Christ? Yes, it looks unlikely, but Jesus comes back to his Father as one with sinful humanity, very tired and battered from his time with us; and the Father welcomes not only his Son but also all his weary sisters and brothers along with Jesus.

And the image that speaks to me of Christ's own love is the love with no strings he shows on the Cross. We look at the Cross and see the perfect image of the unseen God. We look at the Cross and see Light from Light; we see that God loves us even when we crucify him; we see Jesus making excuses for his murderers; we see Jesus' last will and testament, a statement he will never go back on; we see the thief forgiven even when there is no time left to put his life in order. And we see Jesus holding to this true image of his Father even though it is costing him his life, and even though he had prayed most earnestly to have such a chalice removed from him. Jesus is there the perfect mirror, showing God's love for each last one of us and showing it with crystal clarity.

Chapter Seven

AGE 56–59

While I was writing my own faith-story as *The Other Side of the Mountain* another pattern began to emerge, which was not the same as the seven stages but which did complement the seven. Looking back so long as was needed to write the book and without re-living the years too deeply, I noticed that after each time in hospital I had come out desperately depressed; then by a year or two later I was fine; but then I grew either over-excited or full of panic, in both cases losing my sense of proportion. And so, back to hospital where they took the wind out of my sails and left me depressed all over again. Talking one day with Dr Harry Egdell the psychiatrist who had volunteered to look after me back home, round about the time the faith story was complete, it seemed that I could put my various moods on a scale numbering 0 to 10.

I could imagine a state of depression even worse than those I had experienced, and I called that 0, Zero. Suicidal. Then, clinical depression short of suicidal would be 1. A state of shock after a bereavement, or any state where I could just about look after myself but not cope with a proper job, would be 2. Continuous Monday-morning feeling would be 3. Slight depression would be 4. Perfect balance would be 5. Slight strain would be 6. Uncomfortable strain would be 7. Strain that threatened to go out of control into a panic or manic state would be 8. Strain out of control but not yet obvious to others would be 9. Complete loss of control obvious to all would be 10. Zero and 1 would refer to clinical states; at the other end of the scale 9 and 10 would also be clinical states.

It seemed to me that my coming out of hospital coincided with the movement up and away from Mood 1; then in the following months I slowly moved up through Mood 2 to Mood 3 to Mood 4. For a shorter or longer time I stayed at Moods 4 or 6, then feeling confident again I would take on too much or too many tasks … and start spiralling up into the numbers 7 to 10, then be taken to hospital, where I would be brought down to the bottom again. The secret evidently was to find ways of getting out of the doldrums and up to Moods 4 to 6, but then whenever I found myself trying too hard or imagining I had to hold up the sky or otherwise getting carried away (that is to say, when I found myself at Mood 7 or Mood 8) to slow down and aim for Mood 5 again. Once the dangers of the high numbers became clear to me, I could see the measures to lessen tension as being something desired by God. They are fairly well-known measures, but people of good will are reluctant to see them as called-for by God, so they are slow to use them. They prefer to work on as ever, afraid of being labelled soft and lazy, whether by themselves or by others.

Eventually I wrote it all up in a Christian book called *Finding the Still Point*, and one way in which the Christianity clearly showed through was like this: when I am very low in the moods, I think I am rubbish, but in fact I am not rubbish, I am God's child; when I am too high I think I am God, but in fact I am not God, but only God's child. Knowing myself to be a child of God, and acting accordingly, is the same as 'finding the still point', finding the perfect balance, finding Mood 5. *(See Diagram 4, p. 112.)*

This balance is what keeps me, or anyone, most firmly attached to the magnet which is Christ, with the Spirit, the magnetism, flowing through me. First comes the Spirit from the Father, saying I am not by any means rubbish, since I am God's own beloved son or daughter, uniquely loved. Then once I have been lifted from the floor as far as Mood 5 by this wonderful truth, I am invited by the Spirit to be active in spreading God's work, but as an under-shepherd or a sheepdog, not as one in sole charge of operations. Therefore when I find myself in the mood numbers 7 or higher, God wants me to lean back in the opposite direction. Once again we are with the two big lessons, the two chasms that have to be crossed in St Teresa's mansions: first to believe I am loved with no conditions; then to leave the ultimate planning of the future to God, especially when life seems to be coming badly unstuck again. The old moral dictum about *agere contra*, to 'go against' turns out to be not a case of going against my wicked passions but to be a two-fold watchfulness. When I am low, to go against the low and move upwards in some appropriate way as far as I can; when I am into the high numbers, to go against that in turn, and take steps to ease off. In other words, the business of discernment, of finding out what God wants and then doing it, is the same as the business of adjusting my moods to find Mood 5 and to stay as close to that as possible. This is the best compass course to steer; it is not a self-centred operation, since it is centred on God as both my upholder and my restraint.

The Trinity is completely involved in all this. Only the Father who invites me to call him *Abba* can give me total love from the very source, sending his Spirit to tell me so. Only the Son who gives me his gift of love-in-return can send love back to God in gratitude through me. The first teaches me that I am anything but rubbish and builds up my self-esteem; the second enables me to love to my maximum, without confusing my maximum with God's maximum. To be at Mood 5 or the still point is not inertia, it is something like a yacht reaching through the sea with full sail under a strong and perfect wind, but ready to reef in or take shelter if a storm comes.

I am not trying to rewrite the book *Finding the Still Point* here. It is still out there in print as I write, and I am perfectly happy with it. In this present book I am gathering passages and messages from previous books of mine that deal with the movements of the Trinity in our lives, and this matter of moods is central to my understanding of those movements.

In the course of writing about the still point I found a very fitting place for something I have mentioned earlier. In the Gospels there are sheep and shepherds, people enlightened and people being lights for others, fish and fishers, coins and coin-seekers, people lost and people finding them. Suddenly it became clear that here were the Gospels illustrating the very truths I had discovered for myself about moods. When I am very low, God treats me as his lamb and wants me to know I am loved even if I never do another useful deed in my life. Once I begin to perk up again, the Spirit urges me to try and shake off the lethargy and join in with a bit of shepherding. I reach a balance in my life. If then I start taking on too much, the Son reminds me that I am not God, only God's son or daughter (not the Great Shepherd, only an under-shepherd or a sheepdog), so to go a bit easier for the best results. If I ignore that invitation and push myself to an extreme, the Spirit blows me back in one way or another; one way or another, the Spirit takes the wind out of my sails.

In the low moods and the over-high moods, there is a time for effort and a time to slow down. A long time ago, I was given two pottery 'peace doves' from El Salvador by two friends of mine who were working there. These little doves hang on cotton strings in my room, one facing me and the other facing away. The dove facing me is the dove of my baptism, cheering and encouraging; the dove flying away from me is the dove of my confirmation, the dove of my transfiguration, inviting me to follow and live a life of service. When I need lifting off the floor, or when I need to remember to leave more to God, then the dove looking at me is the best one to watch. When I am being lazy, or equally when I am in danger of going over the top, I need to watch the dove flying away from me, asking difficult things of me out of gratitude to God. It is the same Holy Spirit, but the effect is different when the Father sends the Spirit to me to comfort me (dove facing towards me), as opposed to when the Spirit is going back from the Son, or from the son or daughter, to the Father and effort is needed (dove facing away from me). By any reckoning the Spirit coming to me with all God's love is the most vital movement of the Spirit, because unless the Spirit comes to me I cannot be inspired by it or pass it on to anyone else. I am not the source of the wind; only if the wind comes to me first, can I as a mere flute or piccolo play a tune.

Thus the dove coming towards me with infinte love takes the following forms in the gospel images:

I am God's beloved **lamb,** the one-in-a-hundred sheep
  The **light** of God's undying love **shines on me**
God will see **this little child** safely across life's dangerous road
  I am God's beloved **son or daughter**
God's unshakeable love for me is **my rock**
  I am a little **fish** caught in God's net of baptism
God's image is on me, this **coin,** because I am God's precious child
  God will make **the field** that is me fruitful, God will sow seed
God will guide me, through Jesus whom he has sent
  Like Martha's sister **Mary** I listen to Jesus before I act
Even **Jesus was baptized,** his baptism a model of mine
  My baptism celebrates unconditional love from my Father
Jesus feeds me with **bread beside the water,** no entrance fee
  All these priceless gifts are **free**
I am unconditionally **forgiven,** I need only ask for forgiveness
  I am **God's beloved child,** in whom he is well pleased
The **Spirit proceeds** from the Father **to me** with endless love
  All this is given; I need only believe it (= **faith**)
To let myself be loved is **essential, but costs nothing**
  The Spirit here works like **water,** cleansing, lifegiving, soothing.

There is a corresponding gospel image to all of these, on the active side of the Spirit's work in us. We could think of it as being invited to show our gratitude to God by repaying in kind: God shepherds me the lamb, and when I know what it is to be loved as a lamb I go out and shepherd somebody else. When the beautiful light has shone on me, I polish my mirror and shine it on to someone else. *(See Diagram 5, p. 113.)* People of good will need to remember that all of the images on the second list that follows are indeed secondary: unless the Spirit first comes to me from the Father to teach me what it is to be a lamb of God, I will never learn to be a good shepherd.

The lamb becomes a **shepherd** but is still a lamb
   The enlightened one as a mirror reflects **light for others**
A little child, being led by God, has **power** to lead others
   The son or daughter, out of gratitude, acts as a **servant**
Based on the rock of God's love, I can be a **rock for others**
   The fish becomes a **fisher**, but remains a fish
The coin becomes a **coin-seeker**, searching out God's image
   The field once sown with seed becomes **fruitful**, a **sower**
Once I have been shown the way, I can become a **guide**
   As **Martha** was slow to learn, I must learn, to listen
   first, then act
From lamb to shepherd, fish to fisher, I am **transfigured**
   Confirmation is a voluntary sacrament, to show
   gratitude
The **wine** is a gift to inspire the foolishness of the Cross
   This side of the Gospel is **costly**
It involves **forgiving** all others
   I am still God's beloved, but God wants people to **listen
   to me**
The **Spirit calls me** to love God with no conditions, in
return
   Love has grown out of faith, and love is not easy
Love is **voluntary**, there are no measures
   The Spirit here works like **fire**, with joy, life, sparkle
   and risk

In other words, the movement illustrated in my *Diagram 1*

(p. 109) is not only a picture of how Jesus speaks of things within the Trinity, it is also a picture of what happens in us as and when we become united with Jesus. I will leave the two sides of the Gospel for now: the ideas went into another book, *The Two-Edged Gospel,* which would better have been called *The Two Sides of Good News*: I think the reading public is not too attracted by sharp edges! Yet the book has been very popular in the place where I work, since retreatants often come to us overburdened, and in the book they find twenty ways of coping with their burdens, all based in the Gospels.

As part of the scope of *The Two-Edged Gospel* I did bring in frequent references to the Trinity. In fact when I first set out to write it I wanted to call it *He and She and It and God*, but for reasons unconnected with the Trinity it was turned down by the adviser appointed by the Jesuit superior to vet it. The reasons were to do with my rather hopeful guesswork about the origins of the image of God in history and pre-history. Hence, this time round, I am writing strictly about the present, and my experience of God, and my experience of what is said in the Old and New Testament and the early Christian writers, and going no further back than that.

Round about this time in my story, an old familiar way of praying began to take on special meaning for me. From an early age I had spoken in my heart to Holy God, and then when that collapsed, Miss Higham had revived it as talking to Jesus instead of talking to myself. Now having as it were reached the summit of my 'Rock of Gibraltar' climb and coming down the other side, I found myself talking familiarly to the Father again, who had run to meet me, and somehow losing Jesus as the constant companion. It was like coming home before actually arriving home, and it was something Jesus seemed to want, as we read in the Gospels how he constantly pointed himself and his disciples towards his Father. Jesus, it seemed to me now, had gone on ahead to prepare the supper for my Father and me in readiness for our arrival after our long walk back down the mountain.

Call it, if you will, the second coming of Christ seen as Christ there in readiness and my coming to him with his Father. Again Jesus is the forgiving elder brother instead of the judgemental one.

The special difference was this. If I can talk to God with total familiarity, as anybody can if they want to, and if nobody else can hear, then it follows that God and I can see the same scene at any given moment. Nobody else knows in exact detail what the world looks like from where I am standing, even if they are standing beside me. Nobody else knows what the sounds in my ears sound like, not exactly, even if they are in the same room. Nobody else knows what it feels like to feel the sadness or tiredness or joy or peace or anxiety I am feeling at this moment. I can tell them about it, and they can make a guess from their own past and present experience, but they are only guessing. There is only God who knows **exactly** what I am looking at at any given moment, and what it is that I am sharing with God at that moment. Only God and I know **exactly** what the inside and outside world sounds like to me at any given moment. If sights and sounds stir memories in me, only God knows and remembers at the very same moment. My vision, my hearing, my feelings, my memories are real, they are part of reality. And every reality is underpinned by God. I could not see unless God was there seeing what I see, and so on to the other experiences. I could not feel unless God was feeling with me. The world out there is real, and all human beings share it, along with the other creatures. But there is a different and added reality hidden in the experience of each human being and each creature, and that is where we have our unique relationship with God, different from anyone else's. One world, many windows.

What it comes to is this: I need never be lonely, since God is inside me, looking out with me through my unique window on the world, listening to the sounds I hear, knowing **from the inside** the feelings I have at any moment. This is only a logical conclusion from the fact that I can pray moment by moment to God and be sure God knows just what I am talking about. Yet somehow to say, 'Only God and I can see what I am seeing at this moment' is a step forward, and one I had not taken until now. Or rather, it is best to say, 'Only you and I, Holy God, can see exactly what I am seeing at this moment.' How could I ever be lonely again after such a realisation?

We often speak as if the coming of God the Son into the world was the best proof we have that God knows and cares about the way we feel and all the other things that are happening to each one of us. But it has always seemed to me there was a flaw in the argument. Jesus knows from experience what it is to be human, what it is to suffer and be crucified, but he does not know from experience what it is to be confined to a psychiatric hospital. On the 'Jesus once walked the earth' reasoning, he only knows what he knew. My clear conclusion from the new insight about God looking out through my eyes with me, is that this closeness with God has always been true ever since the Creation, but we only dared to believe it once Jesus had arrived among us.

Another most consoling thought that came to me around this time was that if, as the old Catholic philosophers and theologians say, God is simple, and God cannot be divided up into parts and be partly here and partly there, but must be completely there wherever God is ... then I have God's complete attention all the time, and I can speak to God within me confident that he is not so busy with the stars that he has no time to listen properly to me. This again is something I must have known as a little child, confident that God could spend however long it took to give me a personal tour of the universe, without inconveniencing anybody else.

Yet another comforting thought was this: God has no favourites, so therefore everyone is just as much God's favourite as everybody else. Peter and Paul both assert that God has no favourites, and the first reaction on hearing such a statement is one of disappointment, since each of us in our own heart wants to be God's favourite. But then on reflection it becomes clear that God cannot favour anyone else above me: not Peter or Paul, not Mary Magdalene, not heroes of today nor saints of today, not even God's own Son. God did not hold back his own Son as being too precious to risk for the likes of me, but sent him to tell me how much I was loved even though in the event it cost that Son his life. In that sense we are all 'first-born sons' as it says in the Letter to the Hebrews (12:23): we are all loved as much as the actual first-born, Jesus.

This awareness of God looking out through my eyes, the immanent God who is just as truly within as the transcendent God is seeing me from the outside, is not an easy gift to hold on to. But I am still learning, and hoping that practice will make perfect. My own experiments with looking at life this way mean that I can only imagine it possible with one Person of the Trinity at one time. Today I look out with the Father. Climbing the mountain with Jesus, I looked at the world with Jesus, whether I thought of it that way or not. And as a child, it was with the Father that I looked out. I see no reason why someone else should not look out with the Holy Spirit in mind. I find it hard to think of looking out with the whole Trinity of Persons. To me it seems more logical to look out with the Father and see Christ everywhere; or else to look out with Christ and find God in all things. That to me is the solution to the puzzle I faced quite early on in my Jesuit life, when I was a Junior in London. How could Christ be within me and also out there? It actually becomes easier to envisage if we think of the Trinity. Either way is valid: the Father is in me, loving Christ out there in all others especially the most needy, and the Holy Spirit goes from Father to Son; or else Christ is within me, and God is there in every other person and creature out there, and the Spirit of Christ works for God-in-creatures out of gratitude.

Chapter Eight

AGE 60–62

Round about these years, I was going through a time of resisting a current among some contemporary Christians in general and Catholics in particular. There was coming to the fore a desire to include the feminine or the female in the image of God more obviously. Although it is agreed that God the First Person is neither a man nor a woman, there seemed to be a permanent bias towards calling God 'He'. So now some were for calling God 'She', or else 'She' as often as 'He'. Others were for leaving gender pronouns out of it altogether and calling God nothing but 'God'. Others like to introduce their formal prayers, 'O God our Father and our Mother . . .' and end as usual with 'through Christ our Lord.' Calling God 'He' was seen as an injustice to women, and the implication was that Jesus should really have known better than to perpetuate such a notion by calling God his Father. Others again like to call the Holy Spirit 'She' while retaining 'He' for Father and Son.

With all this going on among friends and colleagues of mine, and in view of my own love for each Person of the Trinity and for the Trinity, I naturally had to see where I stood about calling any of the three Persons 'He' or 'She' or, for that matter, 'It'. My first and foremost stand is on the word of Jesus. I refuse to think that Jesus Christ, Son of God, my Saviour, was blind and benighted on this subject.

If he calls God his '*Abba!*', then there must be a reason which has nothing to do with God's using male dominance as a model. So, one should look for a reason, a compelling reason, a reason important enough to override any prejudices later generations might read into his word. I have found at least one which satisfies me, and so I go on here to gather the evidence.

The starting point for me was in the way Jesus, in the language of the Gospels and in the New Testament tradition, allowed only one Father for himself and for his disciples, but many mothers. I have already noted where Jesus promises a hundredfold of mothers, but not of fathers. He is surrounded by disciples who are his brother, his sister, his mother but not his father, because he has only one Father, and so do they. His Father and theirs is to be found in his heart and in theirs. So where does this 'one Father, many mothers' fit in with the rest of Jesus' gospel teaching?

I think for a Christian the clue is in the Nicene Creed which we all agree upon, East as well as West on this point. That Creed calls Jesus 'Light from Light.' Jesus is not the source of the light, but the mirror of the light: in our world we look at Jesus to see what the light looks like. Jesus is the light of the world because with his two natures he mirrors the eternal light into our world for the first time. Jesus on the Cross forgiving his enemies and admitting the Good Thief to come with him to Paradise, is showing us what God is like: God the origin – God the First Person. Christ Jesus is the Second Person, showing us what the First Person is like. The First Person is the light that nobody lit. The First Person is the first cause that nobody caused. The First Person is the burning bush, the fire that nobody lit. The First Person is the Rock with no foundation outside itself. The First Person is who the First Person is. The First Person is the love that nobody loved first, that nobody else loved into being.

The cause that nobody caused. That takes us back to St Thomas Aquinas and his Five Ways of showing there must be a God. An endless sequence cannot explain itself, there has to be a cause at the beginning or underlying. In the image of light, there is for Jesus one light, namely his Father, but many mirrors, of whom he himself is the first mirror. He alone is the true reflection. To speak of light is to use a metaphor, and a more accurate image is that of love. God the First Person is the love that nobody loved first. Jesus is love-in-return-for-love, light from light. There is only One who loves entirely before and apart from ever having been loved. If God loved Jesus or if God loved us because of our devoted service, then we would be creating love in God, which would be nonsense. There had been examples of selfless love in world history before, like the Marathon runner who gave his all to bring good news of another kind, yet they are all examples of people who had experienced love before showing love.

But Jesus was telling us that God is unconditional love, that the origin of all things is love with no conditions. Jesus himself is then situated in the Trinity as love-in-return-for-love, the Second Person. The ancient world had reached a notion of God or the One as the origin of wisdom, truth, beauty, justice and such, but had never seen gratitude as something divine in our world, demanding a presence in the Godhead. Recently I checked an index of the collected dialogues of Plato. Thanks or thanksgiving never got a mention. Gratitude is mentioned once, as being most felt by the destitute. Any mention of praise could be to do with flattery. Reverence gets a few mentions, but there is no question of sublimating it as Plato sublimates justice or beauty. Security is only mentioned under the aspect of finance. Trust is mentioned not at all. Yet Jesus Son of God is all of these things: gratitude to his Father, thanksgiving, praise, reverence, trust in the love given by his Father, and security in that love. It did not occur to the ancient philosophers that love is incomplete without a return. God for the Christian is a God whose love is requited in the end.

Next I might say something about why the three Persons of the Trinity are given numbers. Again the clue is in the status of Jesus, as the one who loves as he has been loved.

'As the Father loved me, so I have loved you.' Logically the one who starts the love going has to be the First. Otherwise there would be no love to return. Otherwise there *could* be no love in return. Logically then, the one who loves in return must come Second. The Spirit can only be Third, logically, because until the love has reached from First to Second and then all the way back again, the place of the Spirit is not defined. In God, homesickness demands a homecoming. This is a matter of logic, not of time. Even the Trinity is logical as understood by us children of God. From all eternity God is unconditional love gratefully received and safely returned ... in that logical order. The order has nothing to do with male dominance, 'father knows best' or any such.

Next I would ask my reader to look again at my *Diagram 3 (p. 111)*. At the top is the flow of love if we imagine it confined to the Trinity, apart from the story of creation. The First Person loves with no conditions about having to be loved in return. (The Spirit proceeds from Father to Son.) The Second Person accepts the love, which generates in the Second Person love-in-return. Love begets love-in-return. (The Spirit proceeds from the Son.) The risk that perhaps the love would never come back was a risk worth taking. The risk that the love given in return would not be appreciated also turned out to be a risk worth taking. In Jesus' story of the Prodigal Son the father of the boy risks losing his son for ever when he lets him go with his inheritance, but out of unconditional love he lets him go. The boy also risked being rejected when he came back home empty-handed, but he took the risk and made the journey. In God, both the First and the Second Person are taking an infinite risk all the time, and it is eternally paying off.

But what I wish further to point out in *Diagram 3* is that here we may also have the clue to what Jesus means by our having only one Father but many mothers. There is, as it were, one light of love that moves from left to right in the diagram for *The Trinity*, then back again from right to left. When it comes to the new creation, what I have there called

outreach, there is, as it were, one light that shines on the
Second Person; it reflects back to the First Person and then
also through Jesus' human nature it shines as a divine
mirror on to the disciple, then still the same light on to
another disciple, and another, and so on till all the earth is
full of the Spirit. One light, many mirrors. One Father,
many mothers. As a simple picture from anybody's understanding of sexual love, the one light is what penetrates the
second person or persons from outside and makes them
fertile. Without the divine mirror the Father could not be
fruitful; the fruitfulness happens in the Second Person, but
it could not happen without the First Person. This situation
moreover is irreversible. There is no comparable metaphor
by which one could call the First Person Mother and speak
of one Mother and many fathers. I think it is more than
clear that this latter is not what Jesus had in mind.

What it comes to is this: Jesus is isolating and defending
God as the One who loves for no reason at all, unconditionally, no 'ifs', no 'buts' no 'only ifs'. Every other person,
including Jesus himself, is loved with no conditions by the
One, then is invited to become a reflection of the One. Mary
the mother of Jesus finds favour with God, by God's choice,
and then brings forth a perfect reflection of the One.
Anyone who is penetrated by the light of the One may turn
like a mirror and direct the one light onto another person
and bring to birth in them another mirror of the One, thus
becoming mother to Christ. My fellow disciples are my
sisters and brothers; disciples I bring into being are my children and I am their mother. I do not penetrate their hearts,
only the One does that.

If we decide to stick too rigidly to 'he' and 'she' and
competition, we will never understand the flexibility of
Jesus' use of metaphor. Jesus himself is mother; everyone
except the First Person is mother. Every man is called to be
mother; every woman is called to be mother. There is
nothing second-rate about being mother. Both 'father'
and 'mother' are images of what is there from all ages in
the Trinity. But there is only one **origin** of 'love with no

conditions'. *That* we can never bring to birth. We cannot bring the unborn One to birth; we cannot cause the uncaused; we cannot love the One before the One loves us. We cannot light the light that has been shining from all eternity, we can only hope to mirror it.

When the light of God penetrates me, and I become this new being, this child of *Abba*, this bread-water-and-wine person, I am in a position to look on another human being who does not know God's love and to mother that same love in them. Any follower of Jesus who does this is child of God, bride of God and mother of Christ, as well as being brother and sister to other followers of Christ and to Christ. In every case there is only one Father, only one light. We are all first-generation children of God the First Person, because there is only ever one light even if it comes to us through a succession of many mirrors. We have the characteristics of God who fathered us and of the many who have mothered us into the being we are. Jesus' use of family metaphors is highly flexible, and we try to pin it down to the battle of the sexes at our peril. The basic premise is, I like any other human being am penetrated from outside of me by God's unconditional love and that can render me fruitful. God is not penetrated from outside by me or anything of mine, to make God fruitful.

I would like now to quote in full a passage from *The Revelations of Divine Love* by the mediaeval mystic Julian of Norwich, as translated by James Walsh, SJ. In Chapter Fifty Eight she writes:

> I beheld the working of all the blessed Trinity. In which beholding I saw and understood these three properties: the property of the Fatherhood, and the property of the Motherhood, and the property of the Lordship, in one God. In our Father almighty we have our keeping and our bliss, in respect of our kindly substance (which is applied to us by our creation), from without-beginning. And in the second Person, in understanding and wisdom, we have our keeping in respect of our sensuality, our restoring and our saving. (For he is our Mother, Brother and Saviour.) And in our

good Lord the Holy Ghost we have our rewarding and our enrichment for our living and our travail: which, of his high plenteous grace, and in his marvellous courtesy, endlessly surpasseth all that we desire.

For all our life is in three. In the first we have our being: and in the second we have our increasing: and in the third we have our fulfilling. The first is kind: the second is mercy: the third is grace. For the first: I saw and understood that the high might of the Trinity is our Father, and the deep wisdom of the Trinity is our Mother, and the great love of the Trinity is our Lord.

Some of what Julian refers to is terminology from mediaeval philosophy, about substance, substantial and sensuality. But quite clearly she has sorted out the Trinity into First Person God the Father, Second Person God the Mother and Third Person God the Lord of love. In another place she speaks of Jesus our Mother feeding us not with milk but with his own self in the Eucharist.

Obviously Julian is speaking of Jesus' role and not of his gender. Jesus does the same for himself when he compares himself to a mother hen attempting to gather her stubborn chicks under her wings (Matthew 23:37; Luke 13:34). I think it would be fair to say that Jesus' reference to the pangs of motherhood in the Last Supper discourse could be a reference to the way he himself was feeling at the time, in birthpangs for each and every one of us (John 16:21).

In the same context, we might remember how Jesus sometimes calls people 'son', or 'daughter' according to the Gospel stories. I think it is fair to say that there is always very good manuscript evidence that Jesus did not say 'my son' or 'my daughter' to anyone, but simply 'son' or 'daughter', namely 'God's son' or 'God's daughter', thus giving the wounded person the key to recovery. If however the lesser manuscripts giving 'my' are still to be trusted, then it could be a gesture of motherly affection, but it could not be Jesus treating himself as in any way father to the afflicted person. St Paul is inconsistent in following Jesus' own way of speaking in this matter. He speaks of being mother to the Galatians (Galatians 4:19) and also to the Thessalonians (1 Thessalonians 2:7f.) but then to the Corinthians he says he was the one-and-only who begot them by the Good News (1 Corinthians 4:15). It was of course the Good News, the light itself, which begot them, rather than Paul, even if he was the original preacher of it in their city. One last footnote before I move on to talk about the Spirit: in the list of the two sides of the Gospel *(Diagram 5, p.113)* there is no mention of 'father'. In the place where one might expect it, opposite 'son/daughter', we find no escape from the word 'servant' instead. Paul writing to the Philippians is quite insistent that the Son does not trade on his divine status but becomes a servant or a slave. The story of the Prodigal Son makes the same progression: son, servant, son, not son-becomes-father.

What then of the Spirit, in this debate about 'He' and 'She' and 'It'? The most popular verdict among my friends would be for calling the Spirit 'She', but I could never agree. I have given up arguing with people about this, because it seems to be a very tender point, the whole business. Writing it in a book seems less likely to upset. These friends would argue that the Spirit is a spirit of wisdom, so therefore the descriptions of Wisdom as a woman in the Bible point to the Spirit being rightly called 'She'. Unfortunately as we have seen, this is not the way the New Testament takes it, nor the earliest Christian traditions. St Paul and the writer of Hebrews call Jesus Wisdom, as do, for instance, Justin and Tertullian. Above all, Wisdom is a mirror, an image, and that suits Jesus, not the Spirit.

On my own picturing, the Spirit has no particular 'spiritual gender'. Coming from God the Father, it speaks with a loving Father's voice; coming in return from 'Jesus our Mother' it speaks with a mother's voice. As described by me in these chapters, the voice from the Father, so far from being strident or dominant, is utterly gentle and undemanding. By definition it lays down no conditions before giving complete love. The voice of Jesus on the other hand is often very challenging, calling us to be brave and unafraid, since we have nothing to lose except our lives! I suggested before that the Spirit is heard most truly when we hold a balance half way between thinking ourselves to be rubbish and thinking ourselves to be be God. I am a child of God, and so the Spirit tells me. I do not trade on the fact, but it remains true no matter what I do or fail to do.

When I wrote about this whole topic first it was to give as the title of a book *He and She and It and God*. Somehow or other the Spirit seems like a personal 'It'. So many of the images used by Jesus were neuter words: spirit, wind, fire, water. He seems to describe a personal force between two people, rather than what we would instinctively picture as one of three persons or three people. By this I mean a separate personal force, like the homesickness I have mentioned so often, identified neither with this person nor with that person but very much alive between them. And as the Father's love is fulfilled, and as the Son is secure at home, so the strength of the embrace lies in the fact that they (so to speak) could have *not* reached a happy ending. They were after all free. Homesickness does not lose its strength when we reach home.

I suppose my main contribution to what may be said about the Holy Spirit lies in the two-sidedness which I have stressed all along. My version of the whole story will only fit with the Western view that the Spirit proceeds from the Father and from the Son. I have seen nowhere else my way of dividing up the gospel images into the two sides, and I think it holds. I also think it shows the two-sidedness of the Spirit running through the Gospel of Jesus. And I am totally convinced of the priority of the left hand side of that diagram, the side that includes 'lamb, enlightened, son, daughter, little fish ... etc.' Without that coming first, there would be no Good News. I am loved eternally as a son or daughter, then called to be a servant, in that order.

As a footnote to the whole question of whether it is right sometimes to call God 'He', I think we should remember that for St Paul it is not a metaphor to call God 'Father', and therefore sometimes 'He', but it is a metaphor to call human fathers 'father'. What God is doing all the time is the reality, love begetting love: what human fathers do in begetting, that is the metaphor (see Ephesians 3:14f.). There is only one Father.

Chapter Nine

AGE 63–64

By this time I had been working confidently as a retreat director for nearly ten years. What with keeping faithfully to prescribed medicine and at the same time watching like a hawk how my moods were swinging, I had kept healthy, and a good deal humbler than previously. One of the hand-outs I found myself using quite a lot with retreatants and others who came for spiritual direction was the page illustrating the seven stages of St Theresa's *Interior Castle*. It helped people to see their failures as part of their progress, while in other ways it also helped those whose world was falling apart, and in a retreat house there are plenty of both kinds of people to be found on any given day. Bit by bit it began to teach me something else too: that the two major crisis points, after Theresa's third mansion and after her sixth mansion, fit in to all sorts of other scenarios popularly used to describe the journey of someone looking for God.

I compiled yet another diagram, *Diagram 6 (p. 114)* to suggest how the moves from mansions 1–3 on to mansions 4–6 and then on to mansion 7 are to be found in some other classic descriptions, descriptions using a three-fold pattern. Theresa herself described her first three stages as being like living an Old Testament life; her next three stages were like living the gospel life up as far as the crucifixion; her final stage was like living the life of the Resurrection or the life of the Spirit. One could say that in her first three stages a person is learning, the hard way, that the Father is not 'like a hard man' but is endlessly forgiving and loving. One could say that in the next three stages a person is learning with Christ that the Christian also 'must suffer and so enter glory.' In the final stage the person lives humbly with God balancing each day as being 'not rubbish, not God, but God's child', letting the Spirit's love for oneself be always given priority over our own love-in-return for God. Thus in the end the classic division of the spiritual life into three stages has a vital link with the Trinity itself. Let me first go through the various versions of 'three stages' I have highlighted in this latest diagram.

If we think of the goal, this side of heaven, as being to live in the present moment, then the first stage is where we gradually learn to forgive the past, handing it over into God's loving mercy. Until the light of the Good News really dawns, the driving force of our attempts to reach God is usually a fear of failure, disguised as a desire for perfection. Until we have failed miserably and found (like Peter) that God still loves us, we are less likely to be able to forget the things in the past that upset us, and equally we have fears for the future lest we fail in the future. Once the Good News dawns, we tend to feel so confident in time, that we think our lives will never go very badly again. When they do go awry, through circumstances outside our own control, then fear is always there: 'Will I be able to cope with this? Why is God allowing this to happen to me his friend? When will it ever end? What has gone wrong? This time I really was doing my best.' Experience is the teacher that brings us through to the third and final stage: 'I have learned that God forgives me; I have learned that God does not let me down in a crisis, but stays with me. Therefore worry is a mistake, and I will stop treating worry as a friend.'

Then there is the ancient way of dividing the spiritual life into the purgative way, the illuminative way, and the unitive way. The purgative way turns out to be not so much a 'purging of my evil passions', as I imagined it to be when

I started out on the journey, but a ridding myself of, or being freed from, any notion that I am the one who saves me. God loves me even though I am a sinner or a moral failure. That is the Good News, and the light that it gradually throws on every corner of my life is at work in the illuminative way. The most stubborn corner of my life that has to be penetrated by the light is the pain and suffering in my life: how does good news fit in there? Can it dawn on me once and for all that God loves me even though I am suffering? Then, thirdly, when a person reaches the focal point, and looks out on life through God's eyes and from God's standpoint, that is the unitive way.

Wells and water are favourite images for the spiritual life. In Theresa's vivid simile, we start out going down to the village to the well, then we rig up conduits and pipes to bring the water to our own house. Then the pump and the pipes burst and cannot be mended. That is the first stage of three: we learn our own inadequacy. The second stage of three involves finding a well in my own house under the floor, but alas it runs dry. The third stage is where the seeker finds deep down an underground stream which never runs dry. As Ignatius of Antioch wrote so beautifully on his way to Rome and martyrdom, 'There is within me now no desire for earthly things, but only a murmuring stream that whispers within me, "Come to the Father".' Each of us might express differently what the stream is whispering, but each of us has deep down a way of looking at God, and of God looking at us, which is unique and which is always there to be found.

Under the image of journeys and mountains, the first stage comes out as finding the true direction, the true path that will take us where we desire to go. Before we find the true path there will be false trails to lead us the wrong way. The second stage will be the effort of gradually, slowly, and with much striving getting there, and often seeming to fail when very near the goal. The third stage is the goal, or the top of the mountain, but from there we do not step off into heaven, but have a journey every bit as long again as that which went before, namely to go home again. Put that in the version which fits Jesus' story of the prodigal, and the first stage is to flail around until we realize what we really want is to go home; the second stage is going home saying within ourselves to our father, 'I will be your servant'; and the third stage is to be met by the father, whereupon the two of us go home together.

Ruth Burrows, whose *Interior Castle Explored* I found so useful, has an image of her own that falls into three stages. In another book of hers, *Guidelines for Mystical Prayer,* she describes three islands, the first of which to my mind corresponds to the purgative way, the second to the illuminative way, and the third to the unitive way. What I found specially interesting was the water between the islands, water that has to be crossed, which I think of as the two major shifts, that of the Good News dawning, and that of the final abandonment into God's Providence before the third island. And also this image of Ruth Burrows' illustrates very clearly that the unitive way is an island, not our final homeland. There can still be troubles in plenty to occupy our time, they just do not cause us the same grief as before.

Then there is my own experience of starting religious life as one following Jesus (stage one), then of being one with Jesus, Jesus using my hands to work with and so on (stage two); and latterly of Jesus going ahead and waiting for me and the Father to come down the mountain and home for the supper (third stage). I have no idea how many or how few other people may have felt these particular changes while going their journey closer to God, but in my own case this was how it felt, as I have already described in these pages.

As for the Spiritual Exercises of Saint Ignatius of Loyola, which as part of my Jesuit formation I have twice been through, these do bear some relation to the three traditional stages of spiritual life. The so-called First Week of the Exercises is purposely focussed on bringing the retreatant to see himself or herself as a forgiven sinner, forgiven once and for all, recipient of the Good News of Jesus. It is quite possible, and often happens, that a mature person will in the course of that week or ten days of prayer be so utterly convinced of God's love and mercy that they will never look back. What happens in the Second Week and the Third Week of the Exercises is mainly a guided tour through the childhood and public life of Jesus up as far as the crucifixion, followed by the Fourth Week which is mainly to do with the Resurrection and the love of God. That might seem to be equating the Second and Third Weeks to the second stage of the spiritual life, and the Fourth Week to the third stage, in line with St Teresa of Avila's view of progress. But of course the second stage, the illuminative way, can and usually does take years, (while the seed grows secretly, while the leaven works through the dough), as also does the move into the third stage and the living of the third stage, living in the present moment with God for as long as it takes. So although the Exercises point out the way ahead for anyone who has been thoroughly turned around by the First Week, nobody would claim that a month of four weeks is enough to bring someone to total unity with God. It may have happened for someone like Francis Xavier, but it does not usually happen so suddenly, nor do the Exercises claim to bring retreatants to the mountain tops in four weeks.

At the foot of my *Diagram 6* I have summed up the three stages as three learning processes: once the first lesson has been learnt, another lesson appears for the learning; once that is learnt, a third lesson appears, which occupies the rest of our life. The first lesson is to believe that God loves us unconditionally; the second lesson is, that even though I do my best and am loved by God, things can go horribly wrong; the third lesson is to carry on doing one's best and ask no more questions of God. I would link the first lesson with the Father in my own case because I started as a child loving the Father easily, then lost contact, then had God's love restored to me through Jesus. I would link the second lesson with Jesus because that is the lesson he had to learn in his life and in his passion; I would link the third lesson with the Spirit because for me that third stage is a constant keeping of the balance between the Spirit blowing towards me with love, and the same Spirit beckoning me on to do great things for God. This is the balance halfway between being rubbish and being God, to put it bluntly, the balance to stay poised in the middle as God's beloved daughter or son, so that the next step to be taken is always the obvious one.

What I have just said about the Spirit coming and going reminds me of another visual aid I took to using round about this time: a metre or so of hosepipe! Held in the shape of a doorway, like Π, it represents resistence to the movement of the Spirit, since the Spirit 'goes in a U shape', as I have hoped to indicate in *Diagram 1*. If I am striving to love God so much that God will have to love me, then I have totally missed the point, just as pumping or blowing water up one end of the hopepipe held thus Π will only for all my effort give me back what I sent up. Whereas the movement of the Spirit is like water of love poured in from above the hosepipe held thus U; this gives us from God endless undeserved love which then flows back up from us to God by God's strength, not ours. Water poured in at one summit flows down, then up and out at the other summit. This I realized is the key to the difference between the Old Testament and the New, since a human servant can never hope to please the divine master in every way and all the time, but a son or daughter can be beloved by *Abba* all the time and whatever happens. So Jesus' one commandment (love one another as I have loved you) is really a double command: first to see how much *Abba* loves me, and then to love *Abba* back by loving one another. The two great commandments of the Old Law simply started from the ground up: Love God with everything you have; love one another ... which proved to be impossible for most mortals. But Jesus' own command can be fulfilled by anyone, because although it demands divine power, the divine power comes to us through our opening up to receive all God gives us and then giving back out of gratitude. We are asked by Jesus to love God back, not to love God by our own strength then hope for rewards. In one of his letters to a benefactor St Ignatius of Loyola once called ingratitude the foundation, origin and source of all sins and of all evil. In his eyes therefore the original sin, namely ingratitude, is the exact opposite of what Jesus came to teach us. Jesus taught us to open our eyes and our ears to the truth he brings and then show gratitude, which is thus the foundation, origin and source of all good.

This latter thought brought me on to considering what, if anything, was wrong with the original creation, that needed so much redeeming? What was the early Christian view of creation? Having been brought up either as Jews or as pagans, in what ways did their view of the beginning of things change once they came to believe in Jesus? My own view may be simple, but I believe it is by no means simplistic. I would return to the visual aids suggested by Jesus himself, namely the bread, the water and the wine. We need to remember that the adding of water to wine was a Greek custom practised also by the Jews of Jesus' time, and that Christian writers as early as Justin referred to the 'commingled cup' when referring to the eucharistic chalice.

Bread is for the human body. Water is for human life. Wine is for the divine life, the Spirit by which we call God 'Abba'. The three words Paul used for the realities were *sôma, psyche* and *pneuma*, in that order. Before Jesus we were bread and water people: there were even early Christian heretics who celebrated the Eucharist with bread and water only, on the grounds that they were unworthy of the divinity: these were condemned because they were in effect refusing the redemption Jesus offered. Bread and water together added up to 'the flesh' (for which Paul's word and John's was *sarx)*. The flesh was weak, but the Spirit made all the difference. The Spirit, in my own visual aid of the hosepipe, turned ∏ into U. 'I am from above; you are from below.' From the beginning, therefore, human nature – bread and water – always had the potential to become divine, just as water has the potential to be mixed with wine and thus become bound up with the wine. All it needs is the presence of the wine, and the mixing.

The prayer from the Mass which I quoted earlier, about the mystery of the water and wine, had a longer version in the centuries before 1966, starting life as an ancient Christmas prayer: 'O God, you have wonderfully established the dignity of human nature, and still more wonderfully reformed it; grant that by the mystery of this water and wine we may become sharers in the divinity of Christ, who humbled himself to become sharer in our human nature.' We were formed as bread and water. Along comes the wine, and we are re-formed as bread-water-and-wine people, like Christ himself. See *Diagram 7 (p. 115.)*

The Gospels themselves, and the New Testament books in general, are full of the idea of creation and re-creation, the weakness of unaided creation and the indestructible strength of the re-creation. The very story of creation in seven days, as found in Chapter 1 of the book of Genesis, is itself upgraded into the week of re-creation by Mark in that earliest of the Gospels. In Genesis the week begins as it were on Saturday evening and ends on Saturday morning, whereas Mark's week of re-creation begins on Sunday evening and ends at dawn on Sunday morning. Mark in effect inaugurated what we now celebrate as Holy Week. Under the wingspread of this idea the Gospels show us how the earliest Christians saw all sorts of things being re-created which by themselves would only have perished. There is a new temple (bread, water and wine) to replace the one that was bound to crumble (bread and water alone); there was a new tree of life, always fruitful, to replace the fig tree which could be caught off-season; there was a new dawn, a new heaven and a new earth to replace the stars that tumbled from heaven and the skies that were darkened; there was the Son who called God 'Abba', obedient and life-giving, to replace Bar´abbas the son of his father, who was a rebel and a murderer.

Over the centuries theologians have argued to and fro, whether God meant us all along to know ourselves as his children, or was it a happy fault on Adam and Eve's part that led to our being upgraded in the fullness of time? Some people are happy to think of themselves as adopted daughters and sons of God, others yearn to be first-generation children from the beginning, only discovering in the course of time who we were all along. If we are adopted, of course, the normal rules of adoption follow: the parents try their utmost to let the adopted child be as much loved as any child of their own. I have already mentioned about God having no favourites, and not even favouring his own only-begotten Son over any one of us that needed saving at that Son's expense. I do not wish to take sides in this debate, being quite content to let God tell me in due course, how it is and how it was and how it will be. But I cannot help recalling my own experience with the story of *The Ugly Duckling* by Hans Christian Andersen. As a child I always thought of it as a miracle story, that an ugly duckling such as I felt myself to be could really turn into a swan. The day it dawned on me as an adult that the 'duckling' had been a cygnet all along was like a minor revelation. So yes, then I looked up the original story and there it was: the egg was bigger than the rest, the mother duck's old neighbour suspected it was a turkey egg and advised her not to hatch it; the description of the ugly duckling matched that of a cygnet, clearly not at home in the farmyard with a clutch of fluffy yellow ducklings. To my surprise, Hans Christian made no secret of the fact that the ugly duckling was really a swan all along: it was my child's imagination that had instinctively preferred the magic jump.

Maybe after all I do have a preference in this debate, though I would not claim to have an unbeatable argument. But if we were from the beginning bread-and-water people, capable of being raised to the status of wine, then that fits in with what I was saying about the need to find the centre of our moods. Perfection for each of us lies at the centre of who we are, yet through all the centuries we were unable to stay there, veering constantly to one side or the other of our true selves, and in consequence under-reacting or overreacting to everything that happened around us. St Paul himself compared the centuries before Jesus to a pedagogy, a primary school education preparing us for adult human life (cf. Galatians 3:23–26). Not until we had the invitation from Jesus and therefore from God to see ourselves as first-generation children of God were we able to find the key to the balance: I am not rubbish, so should not 'rubbish myself' as the saying goes; I am not God, so should not behave as if I am. But at the heart of me I am divine, a divine child of God, and I always was. I now, since Jesus, have always a star that never moves, by which to steer my little craft. This is the story of my life, but it is also the story of the human race. We are all 'chosen in Christ before the foundation of the world' as were the Ephesians to whom Paul wrote.

Chapter Ten

AGE 65–66

Back in my late fifties, as I described above, I was exploring how sharing a permanent window on the world with one Person of the Trinity is a cure for loneliness. This thought has repercussions for how we think about the way the kingdom of God spreads. I remember one of my theology teachers in Dublin once drew two circles on the blackboard, two circles that partly intersected each other. One circle stood for the Christian church and the other circle stood for the kingdom of God. He said the diagram illustrated the fact that many people are in the kingdom who are not in the church, and many people are in the church who are not in the kingdom. Our work as future priests would at least in part be to bring the two circles ever closer. But what has the 'cure for loneliness' to do with the spread of the kingdom?

The emphasis in the Bible throughout the time before Jesus was on 'the people', on rescuing the people from Egypt, on the people's survival in the desert, on the people's finding and winning the Promised Land, on the people having a king or not having a king, on the ups and downs of the people, of their exile, of their return from exile even though reduced to a remnant.

Out of the people came at last the Messiah, the Christ, and his emphasis was quite different. He disapproved of anybody's being excluded from the synagogue or the temple for lack of qualifications. Out on the hillside with Jesus there was no ticket for admission. Even the least of the little ones was not to be despised. As a Christian teacher I can confidently say to any downtrodden person that if they feel the whole world has gone away and left them behind, then they are not alone, since those who exclude them exclude Jesus as well. Jesus died rather than let anyone die alone 'outside the walls'. For Jesus, unless the Prodigal Son is home, there is still work to be done; for Jesus, unless the shepherd has his full tally of one hundred sheep, there is still a search to be made; for Jesus, the family is not home until every little sister and brother of his is home, and he was implacably opposed to those who would exclude the blind, the lame, the deaf, the leper, the sinner, the weak, the under-privileged.

When the joy of being chosen for no reason except God's choice dawns on any one person, they first of all rejoice on their own account. But then comes the realization, 'If God loves me like that, for no merit at all on my part, then God must love my neighbour in the same way and to the same degree!' This thought in turn brings about a completely new attitude to the rest of humanity all around us. We are all blind beggars loved by God, we are all chosen to be younger sisters and brothers of Jesus. The more blind a beggar my neighbour is, wrapped up in sadness or guilt, the more I am impelled to share my joy with him or with her. My prayer goes from *Abba, my Father,* to *Our Father,* rather than in the reverse direction. The one saves the many. One seed to one hundredfold. Jesus saved others but could not save himself, as his enemies, right for once, pointed out. When we know God's love for us we can pass it on and save others, but not otherwise.

St Paul had a fleeting willingness to miss out on his own salvation if only that could guarantee the salvation of his friends in Rome (Romans 9:2), but he quickly, and I suspect with relief, admits that this is impossible. Certainly for myself I would not be in the least interested in any scheme of salvation which saved the whole world and left me outside in eternal darkness. No way. God's way is the exact opposite, to take the most abandoned one into safety, and once I am sure of that for a fact then I will support the cause of the kingdom with all my heart. It is God's personal love for me that is the spur to make me share that kind of love with all others, especially the unloved and the loveless. I know what it feels like to be without it, and I know what unspeakable joy it is to possess it. This is how the seed multiplies, and how the leaven spreads.

All this has to do with the Trinity and its workings. The Son, the Second Person, is loved from all eternity by the Father, the First Person, but the Son is not the cause of the love: the love came freely. Being loved, the Second Person finds it in his heart to love-in-return. The first love begets love-in-return. Moreover, the only-begotten love overflows into creation: 'all things were made through him'. This was a totally free gesture. Christian tradition has always held that God did not have to create us humans. Similarly, as I have been insisting all along, we humans once loved do not stop being loved if we find ourselves unable to share the love we have received from God. Our being loved is a free gift to us; our service of others in return is voluntary. If once I realize with clear sight how much I have been given by God, then inevitably I will want to share with others who are still in darkness, but not everybody has such clear vision, and God's love makes endless allowances.

There was another aspect of my thoughts about loneliness which fits in here. God, according to Christian tradition, is 'simple', as I mentioned in Chapter 7. I have God's complete attention all the time, and I have all God's love all the time. I once made up a story about a golden apple, a fairy story. The golden apple could be divided up into however many slices and still competely satisfy the hunger of however many children. I wrote the story for a mother and father of eleven children, to remind the parents that they might and did have to share the things into thirteen shares, but they could and did give all their love to each of their children. They and their children have never forgotten that story. When we set out to live the life of the kingdom, we find that there is always love enough to go round, no matter how many others we invite inside. As for our not being able to save ourselves, surely it was the love of the Father that kept Jesus going to the end: on the Cross he had reached the end of his own resources. Yet even the Father is not loveless; loving without conditions does not say all there is to say about the Father, even though he was not loved into existence. We can begin to understand from the story of the Prodigal Son that in the Trinity the love freely given comes home in the end, and is more than welcome. By a paradox, it is the very freedom of the love that begets the love-in-return. Jesus made no demands on Zacchaeus, for instance, and if he had, Zacchaeus would have run the other way. Because the welcome was free of all conditions, Zacchaeus gave freely in return. Jesus had learnt from his Father.

Early on in these pages I wrote that the saying, 'In God there are no might-have-beens' is at the very heart of the Trinity. Why is this so? It is because in the Trinity all roads lead home. Homesickness is at the heart of everything. No matter what any of us has done or suffered, there still exists a way home, starting from where we are, and, ultimately, getting home is all that matters. For Peter heartbroken at his own disloyalty, for Jesus on the Cross, life had not come to an end; there is still a way home even from there. When we take our head in our hands and grieve about what has happened, and when we dream about what might have been if only we had done something different, all the time God is not in what might-have-been but is in what is. From where I am now, there is always a way forward, always a way home. Lamenting about the past is a luxury. Well and good, we can learn from past mistakes, and we can tell people we hurt that we are now sorry and try to make it up to them, but the kind of paralysis that can come from brooding about the past is not from God. God has already forgiven. If the people we hurt cannot yet forgive us, that is their problem; God is the truth, and the truth has already forgiven us, with no conditions.

Julian of Norwich takes a couple of paragraphs in her book of *Revelations* to stress that God is never angry. No matter how intently she looked into her visions, she could never see any anger in God. Indeed, it was completely impossible that God should be angry. Our actions deserve that God should be angry, but in fact there is no anger in God. I first came across these sayings of hers many years ago, but in recent years I have looked for ways of squaring what Julian saw with what is written in the Bible. My favourite way was to link what the First Letter of John says about 'God is love' with what Paul tells the Corinthians about the nature of love, thus: 'God is always patient and kind; God is not boastful or arrogant or rude; God is not envious; God does not insist on his own way; God is not irritable or resentful; God does not rejoice in wrongdoing but rejoices in truth; God bears all things, hopes all things, endures all things; God who is love never ends.' When I was first shown this very neat argument, I wrote it out initially for God (the Father) and then also for Jesus, only to find that it did not quite fit Jesus. There were some things Jesus did not seem to be able to bear, like intolerance and hypocrisy; was Jesus always patient with the scribes and Pharisees? Could one say that Jesus was never angry?

My solution to this dilemma is to suggest that the anger of God in the Bible, particularly in the Old Testament, is ultimately the anger of the prophets who see God as being treated without proper respect and with ingratitude. Jesus too as a prophet could get angry at the blindness of those who cheated on God and called themselves virtuous. His Father deserved better than that; his Father was not like the god these people worshipped, far from it. To me it is perfectly believable that God himself is never angry, and it is the prophets and sometimes the Son who are angry on God's behalf. God, the First Person, is total forgiveness, and that is Jesus' final testament on the subject also. He prayed his Father to forgive his murderers, even though they were intolerant hypocrites.

What kind of fruit was Jesus looking for from the temple at Jerusalem, fruit which he did not find? A farmer looks for the same kind of fruit that belongs to the tree or bush that he planted. A father looks for a son or daughter that looks like himself. A while back I listed various ways in which the Gospels picture us giving back to God 'in kind', lamb becoming shepherd to thank the shepherd, fish becoming fisher to thank the fisher, each picture suggesting how to grow into the likeness of the original giver. Paul somewhere asks us to imitate God, and the Gospels put the same request into many different parables and images. The gift of God is unquestioning love, love with no strings, love with no conditions, forgiving love, and that is the fruit God is looking for. God found it in Jesus, there on the Cross forgiving his murderers. Jesus did not find it in the temple when he went looking for fruit on behalf of his Father: instead he found partial love, conditional love, favouritism for the rich and for those few who either kept or pretended to keep the laws and despised everybody else. The fig tree that withered provided a similar picture, of a tree that was only partially fruitful: like our poor bread-and-water humanity, it could not rise to the divine, it could not manage to be fruitful all the time, whenever anyone called upon it.

This whole idea of 'fruit' is linked to homesickness. The Father wishes to gather his own children into his home. In the end, we are ourselves the fruit God wants, as an admission on our part of the truth that we owe everything to God. Once again, gratitude is seen to be the key virtue. Every act of ingratitude is an attempt on our part to say that we are independent, with no roots in God but only in ourselves. Another feature of the difference between good fruit and weeds or poisonous fruit in the Gospels is that the good fruit is 'useful for others', whereas the fruit of the thorns and thistles is either useless or else the plant itself is destructive of good. Selfish love is the anti-God fruit;

unconditional love is God's fruit. Those who in return for God's love love each other without conditions are giving good fruit; but even those who let God love and forgive them with no conditions show they believe in that kind of love even though they find it hard to practise, and it seems this is enough in God's eyes. At the very least it shows true humility.

Many pages ago I promised to return to the fact that Jesus was crucified outside the walls of Jerusalem. This is agreed to be a historical fact; moreover it is used by the writer of The Letter to the Hebrews (13:11–13) to make a point, and it is hinted at in the parable of the vineyard in Mark 12:8. There the murderous stewards of the vineyard took the son and heir and killed him, and cast him out of the vineyard. I have already suggested that since Jerusalem was the beloved vineyard and also the bride of God, this casting out of the seed, the word of God, was a rejection of the marriage bond with God. But God's word is ever fruitful, so the territory outside the city which did receive the seed became the bride instead, namely the whole, wide, unrestricted, universal world ... including Jerusalem, true, but no longer with Jerusalem in prime position, simply as part of the world God loves. The whole world was re-named as a new Jerusalem. What I might add here is that the word in question, the seed, is 'Abba!', and what the city was casting out was the option Jesus gave of anybody and everybody in Israel seeing themselves as first-generation children of God, justified by God and not by their own efforts. The old Jerusalem refused that gift for her children. The authorities and the citizens were not willing to give the fruit back to the one who wanted to be known as their Father nor to let themselves be born again from above. They preferred Bar´abbas, the son of **his** father.

Another place I promised to come back to is the way the Gospels so often point to a shadowy figure behind the main figure in the stories or parables. There is a king who has a son getting married, the owner of the vineyard who has servants but also a son, the farmer who owns the land where the gardener thinks the fig tree could do with more manure, there is the owner of the field who decides not to uproot the weeds yet, in spite of requests for this to be done. In biblical tradition, God is the first Shepherd of the flock: 'I am going to look after my flock myself and keep all of it in view;' and 'I mean to raise up one shepherd, my servant David ...' Jesus is that second David, the shepherd sent by God to do God's work. The sower goes out to sow God's field, not his own field. If we are to be little children, who is the adult to lead us? If we are precious coins to be collected, whose is the treasury? There is even an echo of all this in the very first calling of the disciples James and John. They left their fishing to be fishers for people, they left their father for a greater Father, they left the hired men behind to become free men themselves, they left the boat of their livelihood to trust in Jesus' boat, wherever that might take them. And in the end, says St Paul, even Jesus will hand over the completed kingdom to God the Father. The whole mission of Jesus is pictured in these stories to be that of a son and heir working like a steward of his father's property. Yet at the same time Jesus himself is king, a king subject to his Father but a king. Is he a steward working his way up to be reckoned a king, or a king already, acting like a steward? Obviously for St Paul as for the gospel writers, Jesus is a divine son acting like a steward; the situation is that way round. Jesus is already a king.

So whose is the property? It seems sometimes that the property belongs to this heir, to Christ and his sisters and brothers, already. 'All I have is yours', says the father to the elder brother of the prodigal. 'All things are yours', says St Paul to the Corinthians. We are not waiting for our Father to die. Jesus is the mirror looking always to his Father to check that the image he, Jesus, is giving is the truth. Jesus is the steward of the truth, and the image of the truth. Once we take in the truth that God the great king is our Father, then everything is ours. There are no taxes for the king's children. I look out through my eyes along with God and everything I see is mine, because I see it as it is. I lose my independence but I gain my freedom. My window on the world shows me my principality, I am the prince or the princess and all I see is mine, so long as I remember who is looking out through my eyes with me, the one who gives it all to me.

Over the years I have, like just about everybody else, wrestled with the problem of suffering and the problem of evil. For me the two problems have been resolved through the two major shifts in emphasis I have referred to in previous chapters. When I realized that God loved me in spite of all my faults and failings, I experienced God's forgiveness as stronger than my evil. And if stronger than my evil, also stronger than anyone else's evil. As for where evil came from, my eventual conclusion is that it has nothing to do with devils and hobgoblins, but is simply the result of people having no clear compass (no number 5 on the mood-scale in my language, no clear knowledge of themselves as 'child of God'). With no compass to guide them, they have nearly always over-reacted or under-reacted to situations they met with. The ensuing confusion gets compounded and spirals, it does not simply add one evil to another. Yet from any mess, even the most terrible, there is always, always a way home, through forgiveness. I say this in one short paragraph, but it took many bitter years in the learning.

As for suffering, I either had to alter my understanding of what love is, or else alter my understanding of what 'all-powerful' means when applied to God. I am in dire straits, and I cry to God to get me out of the pain. The pain does not go. So what has happened? Either God is not my friend any more, or else God cannot shift the pain. Now I absolutely refuse to believe that God has turned against me, so where does that leave the situation? No friend, no human friend, would let me stay in pain if he or she could shift the pain. If the pain stays, then the friend is unable to shift it. Now and again there may be reasons why the friend cannot shift it even though I cannot understand the reasons. So for instance a child in hospital might ask his mother to take him home today, today please, but the mother has to leave him there a while to undergo his operation. He might even accuse her, 'Mum, you don't love me any more, or else you would take me home today', which is hard on the poor mother. Similarly, I am sure, God cannot always do today what we ask today. Jesus often said 'With God all things are possible', but when it came to his own suffering, he prayed *'Abba*, Father, if it be possible, let this cup pass from me', and the cup did not pass, but Jesus had to drink it. So it was not possible, not just then. Three days later, yes, but not just then. God will answer our prayers, when the time comes. For Jesus it was three days later; for us it is often longer than that, but it will come, and all will be well.

Evil is personal, that is, evil is only found where persons are found. I believe that without inventing new persons and calling them devils, there are plenty of persons around in history and in the present to account for the evil in the world. Earthquakes on the other hand are not evil, since earthquakes are not persons and they mean no harm. Similarly floods and droughts and forest fires and all such disasters are not evil in themselves, and could only be properly called evil if human carelessness or indifference caused them. There are always unbelievers and wavering believers in God who ask how a God who is love could cause or 'allow' such things to happen. Jesus seems to have taken earthquakes, wars, rumours of wars, famines and various other disasters in his stride, in the sense that he in no way thought they disproved the existence or the lovingness of his Father, and he fully expected them to keep on recurring after he himself had finished his mortal life. The planet earth has a history going back millions of years, and comes as part of a universe that goes back who knows how many millions of years beyond that. The fires within the earth, and the atmosphere and winds and seas and rains and the formation of the rocks and of the soil are what they are, and to say 'Why does God allow earthquakes?', and the rest, is to fly in the face of reality.

Rocks are what they are, one and one makes two, let go of things and they fall to the ground, all these things would be true whatever universe God made. Ultimately we are invited to learn either how to modify our surroundings without causing damage elsewhere, or else so to cooperate with the rest of humankind that we do not let anyone build houses in dangerous places or areas greatly at risk, giving them instead better places to live. No good complaining at snow for falling, or at the sun for shining hot at midday.

For myself, I get upset when people complain and blame God, my God, my beloved Father, for so many things that are not God's fault. God cannot prevent people from having free will, since that is where the human race has arrived after all the millennia. And if we make very poor use of our free will, God cannot interfere, since that would be to deny what we are. But love and forgiveness are still there, ready to heal every single wound in the end. It is not God's fault if germs kill, since germs are part of reality. Who is so all-wise as to say God 'could have created a world without germs'? As I have said earlier, reality is friendly, and there is always an antidote to every harmful thing if we are patient enough to find it. Every generation cures some ills and discovers some others, so each generation of human beings has the same process of discovery to go through, but there is no malice in God. Unless we work on that premise, we never get anywhere. Similarly, forgiveness and love are the only ultimate reality, and if we choose not to be forgiving we have moved into unreality and our personal world will be out of balance until we face reality and accept love and forgiveness. The consequences of making anything but love and forgiveness into our god have been dire, but that is not the fault of love and forgiveness.

St Ignatius of Loyola at the start of his Spiritual Exercises considers it necessary that both the retreatant and the retreat director be determined to take the best possible meaning out of what the other person says. That means, as a general rule we should presume good will on the part of whoever we speak to or listen to, rather than jump to conclusions about their malice. The same would apply to God, in my view. I have so much evidence of love and good will from God; indeed life begins to make sense only when I use that as the starting point. Therefore I hang on to a belief in God's love and wait, whenever difficult things happen to me or to those I love. This I take it is what it means to love God back in the way God loves me, with no conditions, with no strings.

Chapter Eleven

AGE 67–68

This brings me up to the present time of writing, aged sixty-eight. Looking back, I would say that the one sentence in the whole of this book I am most satisfied with is this one, from Chapter 8 above: 'From all eternity God is unconditional love gratefully received and safely returned ... in that logical order.' That to my mind is what the mystery of the Trinity is all about. There is one God: the Father who is unconditional love, the Son who receives that love and is grateful, and the Spirit who makes sure the love gets to its destination, in both directions. Because love has to go from a lover to the loved one, then logically the Father is the First Person and the Son is the Second Person; and because the love-in-return goes back to where it came from, the final moment in logical terms is when the Spirit brings the love back to where it started. Thus the Spirit is logically the Third Person. Because all this is eternally true, always was, is, and always will be, the three Persons are not 'first, second and third' in order of time, nor in order of importance. They are equal in dignity, equal in majesty, equally indispensible to the true and total picture of love.

The young Carmelite Sister, Elizabeth of the Trinity (1880–1906) had this to say about the Trinity: '... the soul thus simplified, unified, becomes the throne of the Unchangeable, since unity is the throne of the holy Trinity'.

She is talking about someone who has simplified life so as to be living only in the present moment, but I think her statement here goes way beyond the immediate case she is writing about. Wherever unity is found, the Trinity is found: in atoms, in electrons, in the movement of the stars, in animals, in families, in the unity which is a live human body, in the one world we live in, as well as in an integrated personality. I am aware that this present book of mine has only looked out at the Trinity through the one window that God has given me, and that every other creature has its own relation to the Trinity, which I can only guess at. But I have no reason to believe that God is anything other than 'love with no strings etc.' anywhere else in the universe. Like Isaac Newton with his apple, there are some truths we just know apply everywhere. Every test we can make proves positive.

'Love' for a Christian means love given with no conditions, then that same love accepted and directed back towards the lover, then safely delivered. Our religion is a story with a happy ending. For each of us life is a pilgrimage, but the God we believe in is one in whom 'all will be well' in the end. We do not believe in a God who demands 'give, give, give' without end, because unselfish love comes back home if we are endlessly patient.

There is always a difficulty of language, which is not too difficult to surmount. I was given the clues to the solution by Father Kevin Smyth, back in my days studying theology. The word 'God' usually refers, in Christian writings and speech, to the One Jesus called his Father. But the word 'God' is sometimes used to mean either the Trinity or another Person of the Trinity. That is because Jesus stretched the image of the godhead into three dimensions: love with no strings, that same love accepted and directed back to the lover, and the safe delivery of the love in both directions, there and back. We can say Jesus Christ is God because without love accepted and love directed back to the lover, there would be no complete picture of love. Likewise if Father loved Son and Son loved Father and they never told one another, never showed one another, the picture of love would be very inadequate. Also without love with no strings the whole movement of love could never get started. So each Person is essential to what God (as seen by Jesus) is, to what the Divine is, to what love is. So Christ Jesus, the Word who says '*Abba!*', is God because God would not be the complete picture of love without him. The Spirit is God because the Spirit alone knows how to communicate love, there and back. (I was conducting a marriage the other day, and it struck me forcibly how vital it is that the couple keep on communicating. Each of them is lover, each is loved, but each needs to know the love of the other.)

I sometimes wonder, these days, if the First Person of the Trinity is the One and only who never thinks of self? Does unconditional love, pure and simple, ever think of self? Two things make me wonder in this way. First, the closer we humans get to what Teresa of Avila calls the seventh mansion, the less we think of ourselves, leaving all the worries to God, who doesn't seem to be worrying either. Secondly, the story of the Prodigal Son seems to depict in the father of the two sons someone who does not think of himself at all. His joy and fulfilment comes in the return, against all hope, of the one he had given his freedom. Self is loved in the Trinity, but the self of the First Person is loved by the love-in-return of the Second Person, or so it seems to me. Jesus takes it for granted that we should love ourselves, but the way the Trinity goes about things seems to show us how it may be done: like Jesus himself we know ourselves loved and therefore lovable, and then are invited to love others as we are loved. I could of course be wrong, but this is how it seems to me. If I am right, then we have another way in which the First Person is our 'only one Father', since neither Jesus nor any other person in the universe or outside of it is completely without self-love. There is only one source of pure unconditional love. As for whether the Spirit is without self-love, I have not even begun to wonder about that one.

'It's just that I'd like to feel that Father really loves me, not because I'm his child, but because I'm me, Anne.' I came across that sentence a short while ago, on re-reading the diary of Anne Frank, who was in hiding from the Nazis with her Jewish family. She was echoing the desire I had as a Junior in London, only in my case the Father was God the Father. Perhaps after all if God the First Person is completely without self-love, then I am loved for my own sake, not even for Jesus' sake, and certainly not for God the First Person's sake.

Another thing: when Jesus speaks about losing ourselves to find ourselves, he means losing our independence, letting ourselves be loved from outside, and then discovering who we really are and where our power really lies. With God the First Person, there is also a losing of self, since the First Person takes a gamble all the time, and loves without any promise of a return. With us, as with Jesus, the guarantee comes first: we are loved, then we are invited to love in return. With the One Jesus calls Father, love goes out first and permanently, before there is any return. In moments of darkness we can do something similar, trying to love when nothing seems to be coming back; but only the Father in heaven actually does it, loves before being loved.

One more astonishing thought has been with me recently. If God the First Person is unconditional love and if the Son is unconditional love-in-return-for-love, then forgiveness is built in to the Trinity itself, and is not simply something brought in for us sinners. In other words, no one, not even God, can really say 'I will love you even if you turn round and hurt me', unless rejection of the love is at least possible. Therefore if God is unconditional love in the Trinity, the possibility of rejection must have been there too. In support of this, I have long thought that Jesus was sinless *because* he understood the fathomless depth of his Father's mercy, and so too we sinners are all the less likely to sin maliciously, the more we realize how good the Good News is. Loving in God's way is nothing like making others walk a tightrope. So many times in our darkness we sin because we are afraid of what may happen if we sin: we lose our nerve because we think we are going to lose God's love, and so we fall.

So all in all, my relationship to the Trinity has ended up where it began, as in all good stories of homecoming. Instead of speaking to myself all day, I speak to 'Holy God' as I did when I was a little boy, only now I do it all day long. In the meantime in my life I have been 'there and back again' with Christ Jesus. Now as I go down the other side of the mountain with God my Father, it is the Holy Spirit who keeps me on my feet, balanced securely between thinking I am God and thinking I am useless.

The last book before this one that I wrote was called *100 Ways to hear Good News*. It contains eighty-five straightforward ways of understanding Jesus' Good News, and then fifteen of what I call 'Ah, buts ...' So often when I preach and teach the Good News in all its glorious simplicity, listeners find it too good to believe. 'Ah, but ...,' they say, 'what about this and what about that?', listing various items of apparently bad news, whether from the Bible or from the rest of life. A lot of my energies nowadays are spent defending the goodness of the good God.

One final refrain: the Persons of the Trinity are eternally equal and equally eternal. I have stressed that the priority of the 'first' has nothing to do with time, since God is in time but timeless. Logically, however, there can be no love-in-return without love being there first, even if the process has been going on for ever and will go on for ever. And the lock between the two loves can only be closed, logically, when the two loves are there and connected.

And they are eternally equal because 'love' whole and entire is not there unless all three Persons are there. The loss of the Spirit would mean endless heartbreak, the loss of love-in-return would mean love was meaningless, and the loss of unconditional love at the heart of reality would mean slavery for anyone and everyone else.

THE FOUR MOVEMENTS OF THE SYMPHONY

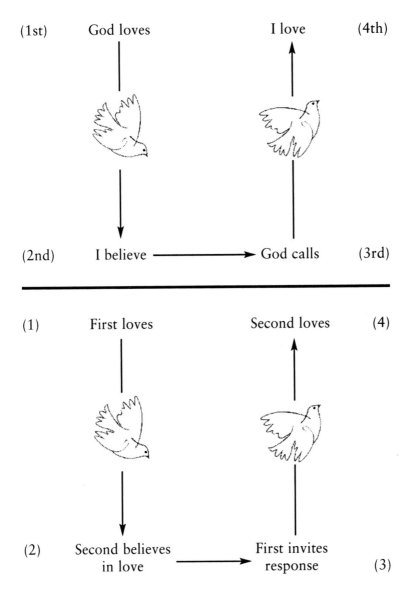

(1st)   God loves   I love   (4th)

(2nd)   I believe ⟶ God calls   (3rd)

(1)   First loves   Second loves   (4)

(2)   Second believes
in love ⟶ First invites
response   (3)

Diagram One: The direction in which the Spirit moves.

SAINT THERESA OF AVILA'S SEVEN MANSIONS

as a model for progress

		... in life	... and in prayer
(1)		Find God deeply attractive	Start trying to pray
(2)		Commitment	Regular prayer
(3)		Commitment is not enough	Prayer 'goes to pieces'
Failure is 'my own fault', but God loves me, this sinner			
(4)		Good News	Glad you didn't stop altogether Pick favourite way(s)
(5)		Prayer and life fit together Confidence grows	More confidence with scripture Confident to teach
(6)		Troubles/difficulty persecution etc.	Praying not so difficult as living
Not my own fault, but God loves me though I am suffering			
(7)		= 'living in present moment'	Having gone through 1,2,3 no worries about the past Having gone through 4,5,6, no worries for the future Thence pray in the present moment

Diagram Two: 'Seven Mansions'.

UNQUESTIONING LOVE

Unquestioning love → *Spirit proceeds* → Love received

Love fulfilled ← *Spirit returns* ← Love mirrored

THE
T
R
I
N
I
T
Y

and Outreach ...
Unquestioning love → *Spirit proceeds* → Love received
(the Lamb)

Spirit returns ←

Good Shepherd
loves with
unquestioning love

Disciple beloved = lamb

Disciple loves in return = under-shepherd

Another disciple loved

This disciple loves
in return

and another, till the Spirit fills the whole earth

Diagram Three: Unquestioning love.

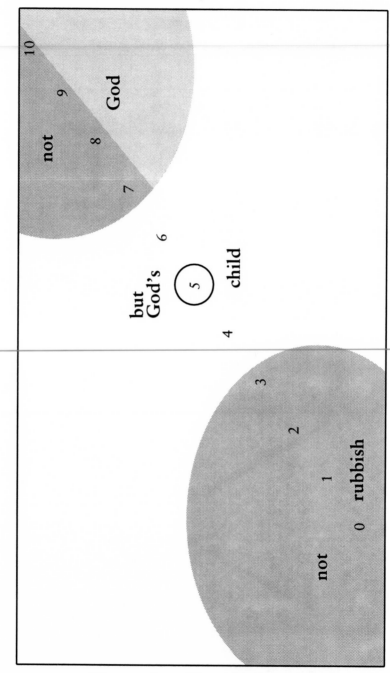

Diagram Four: The scale of moods.

THE TWO SIDES OF THE GOSPEL

First, receiving as free gift	then invited to give in kind
lamb/sheep	shepherd
enlightened	light for others
child	power
son/daughter	servant
built on rock	rock for others
fish	fisher
coin	coin seeker
sown with seed	sower (fruitful)
guided on the way	guide
Mary	Martha
Jesus baptized by John	Jesus transfigured
baptism	confirmation
bread and water	wine and water
free	costly
forgiven	forgiving
'You are my beloved ...'	'This is my beloved ... listen to him/her'
Spirit loves	Spirit calls (invites)
faith is the response	love is the response
necessary	voluntary
water	fire

Diagram Five: The two sides of the Gospel.

PROGRESS THREE STAGES

Before any progress at all, comes the love of God with no conditions. Then,

(1)	(2)	(3)
First Three Mansions	4th to 6th Mansions	7th Mansion of Castle
Worries about past and future	Worries about future only	Living in the present
Living Old Testament life	Living Gospel life	Living life of the Spirit
'Purgative Way'	'Illuminative Way'	'Unitive Way'
Seek the well	A well found, but it dries up	Ever running stream
Seek the path	Climb the mountain	Summit **or** ~~Down the other~~ side and home
Prodigal thinks of going home	Goes home as 'servant'	Met by the father
First Island	Second Island	Third Island
Try to follow Jesus	One with Jesus	One with the Father
('First Week')	('2nd & 3rd Weeks')	('4th Week' of Spiritual Exercises)
These are learning to believe that God loves sinners unconditionally	These are trying their best but learning that God loves them even if they fail or suffer	These do their best and ask no more questions of God
Knowing the Father	*Knowing the Son*	*Knowing the Spirit*

Diagram Six: Progress three stages.

BREAD	WATER	WINE
'made by hands'	'capable of the divine'	'gift from heaven'
human body	human life	divine life
Greek: *soma*	Greek: *psyche*	Greek: *pneuma*
the flesh		the Word
slavery until …		… cries 'Abba!'
One Body	One Spirit in Christ	
Body of Christ	Blood of Christ	

Note: to my mind it is a pity that the current offertory prayer talks about wine as being 'made by human hands' or 'the work of our hands'. The New Testament and other early Christian writers make it clear that wine represents the divine. Add earth to earth and you get earth, but add earth to the divine and you get the Incarnation. Wine is doubtless only a visual aid, but surely it is true that human hands can make grape juice, but they cannot make wine.

Diagram Seven: Bread, water, wine.

APPENDIX: THE THEOLOGY OF THE TRINITY

What the Church believes about the Trinity comes from a combination of four main sources:

1. What the Gospels and the New Testament say;
2. What the earliest Christian writers had to say;
3. What the Councils of the Church put into formulas about the Trinity; and
4. What writers and saints have tried to put into words over the centuries about the Trinity, while remaining true to the first three sources.

This appendix tries to show how my own vision of the Trinity fits in with the formulas agreed by the Councils of the Church. In the course of this book I have already used the Gospels and the rest of the New Testament as my sources, and I have also referred to some of the early Christian writers who followed the first generation. Here then are some of the main themes fixed by the Councils.

The Trinity is a mystery. Natural reason cannot entirely grasp it even when it has been revealed. Anyone who has read my book so far will realize that my way in to the Trinity is not getting much further than the gateway, but the view from there is wonderful.

There is one indivisible God. In my book, there is only

one Love, in no way lessened by there being three Persons.

Within the Godhead there are two 'processions'. The Father begets the Son ... Love with no conditions begets love-in-return-for-love ... *and the Holy Spirit is breathed forth by the Father and the Son as from a single source (added by Western Councils from 2nd Lyons (1274) onwards, with an interpretation at Florence (1493) designed for acceptance by the East).* The Holy Spirit goes in two directions, from Father to Son with unconditional love, and back from the Son to the Father in gratitude.

These two processions are outside the conditions of space and time. They happen all the time in our world, but are not subject to space and time.

There is no priority, or seniority, or inequality betweeen the Persons, but there is a movement from the origin – see below. I have tried to explain more than once in my book what is meant by First, Second and Third Person, and that it does not imply priority or seniority or inequality. If any one Person of the Three was missing, there would be no good God.

It is the common opinion of theologians that the Son proceeds from the Father in some sense through understanding, and that the Holy Spirit proceeds from the Father and the Son through will. The nearest to that in my own book is that the Son must understand how utterly he is loved by the Father; the Holy Spirit on the other hand moves the lover and the loved one to action, at least in our world so perhaps in some sense within the Trinity itself.

Because of the two 'processions' there are four relationships within the Trinity:

1. *that of the Father to the Son* ... unconditional love;
2. *that of the Son to the Father* ... love-in-return-for-love;
3. *that of the Father and Son to the Holy Spirit;* and
4. *that of the Holy Spirit to the Father and Son.*

There is only one breath, breathed out on one side as it is taken in on the other, or breathed back from the other and taken in by the first. To use an over-simple picture, it is like two wings of a butterfly relating to the one body between, or the one body between relating to the two wings.

The whole reality of the three Persons consists in their relationships to one another. It is the way in which together they tell the whole story of love which shows what we mean by 'Person'.

The Trinity is **not** *like an actor putting on three different masks or 'faces'.* That would give us one person in God, with three different roles.

There is only one divine Essence. That is to say, only one true version of love, which must include total forgiveness. Love would not be unconditional unless there was a chance of its **not** being returned, in which case forgiveness would then be called for.

The Father is identical with the divine Essence. The Father is identical with love and forgiveness. *The Son is identical with the divine Essence.* The Son is identical with love and forgiveness. *The Holy Spirit is identical with the divine Essence.* The Holy Spirit is identical with love and forgiveness.

And yet the Father is not identical with the Son or the
   Holy Spirit,
  the Son is not identical with the Father or the Holy Spirit,
  the Holy Spirit is not identical with the Father or the Son.

There are two wonderful words used for the way the Three are described as being in One, namely *circuminsession* and *circumincession*. The first is a technical term for the way Jesus says 'I am in the Father and the Father is in me' (John 14:11), or else that the Holy Spirit knows all the thoughts of the Father and the Son (compare John 16:14f.). A more familiar word for this is 'indwelling'. *Circumincession* is coined to suggest movement, which I have tried to indicate in my various diagrams, especially the one about the direction of the Holy Spirit, which might be described as circular, but going strictly in one direction only (i.e. 1. First loves, 2. Second believes, 3. First invites response, 4. Second loves, as in *Diagram 1*).

In any activity outside the Godhead (creation, conservation, redemption) the three Persons act as one. No one Person acts before, after or without the other Persons (Council of Toledo). Thus St Ignatius pictures the Trinity deciding upon the means of our redemption, even though only the Second Person was made flesh and died for us. *In God 'everything is one except where this is impossible because of reciprocal relationship' (Council of Florence).* So, for an obvious example, the Son does not beget the Father.

Note:

The sections in italics in this appendix depend largely on the summary in *The Theology of the Trinity* by Laurence Cantwell SJ, Cork, Mercier Press, 1969.

SOME BOOKS I HAVE FOUND USEFUL

Andersen, Hans Christian, *Fairy Tales,* Ware, Wordsworth Editions, 1995.

Bettenson, Henry, *The Early Christian Fathers,* Oxford University Press, 1990.

Burrows, Ruth, *Guidelines for Mystical Prayer,* London, Sheed and Ward, 1990.

——, *Interior Castle Explored,* London, Sheed and Ward, 1985.

Cantwell, Laurence, *The Theology of the Trinity,* Cork, Mercier Press, 1969.

De Rosa, Peter, *God our Saviour,* London, Geoffrey Chapman, 1967.

Elizabeth of the Trinity, *Complete Works,* Washington DC, Institute of Carmelite Studies, 3 vols, 1984 onwards.

Howell, Clifford, *Mean what you pray,* Collegeville, 1965.

——, *The Work of our Redemption,* Tenbury Wells, Fowler Wright, 1975.

Irenaeus, Saint, *The Writings of Irenaeus,* Edinburgh, T. & T. Clark, 3 vols, 1868.

Ivens, Michael, *Understanding the Spiritual Exercises,* Leominster/New Malden, Gracewing/Inigo Enterprises, 1998.

Justin Martyr and Athenagoras, *The Writings of* ... Edinburgh, T.& T. Clark, 1870.

Jeremias, Joachim, *The Central Message of the New Testament*, London, SCM Press, 1965.

'Joint Lutheran-Catholic Declaration on the Doctrine of Justification', in *Briefing* (official documentation of Bishops of England and Wales, vol. 29, issue 11, 10 November 1999).

Julian of Norwich, *The Revelations of Divine Love*, James Walsh (tr), Wheathampstead, Anthony Clarke, 1980.

Kelly, J.N.D., *Early Christian Doctrines*, London, A. & C. Black, 1993.

O'Mahony, Gerald, *'Abba! Father!'*, Manila, St Paul, 1987. *(Or from Loyola Hall, £4.00 incl. inland postage.)

——, *The Cup that I drink*, Gujarat, Gujarat Sahitya Prakash, 1999. *(Or from Loyola Hall, £4.00 incl. inland postage.)

——, *Finding the Still Point*, Guildford, Eagle, 1993. *(Or from Loyola Hall, £6.00 to within the U.K.)

——, *The Other Side of the Mountain*, Fisher-Miller, 1997. *(Or from Loyola Hall, £5.00 to within the U.K.)

——, *Praying St Mark's Gospel*, Gujarat, Gujarat Sahitya Prakash, 1999. *(Or from Loyola Hall, £6.00 to within the U.K.)

——, *The Two-Edged Gospel*, Guildford, Eagle, 1995. *(Or from Loyola Hall, £3.00 to within the U.K.)

——, *100 Ways to hear Good News*, Buxhall, Stowmarket, Kevin Mayhew, 2000. *(Or from Loyola Hall, £8.00 to within the U.K.)

——, *The Way of the Cross*, Liverpool, Metropolitan Cathedral, 1995. *(Or from Loyola Hall, £4.00 to within the U.K.)

——, *Do not be afraid*, Buxhall, Kevin Mayhew, 1999. (Or from Loyola Hall, £10.50 to within the U.K.)

——, *Simply Free*, Buxhall, Kevin Mayhew, 1997. *(Or from Loyola Hall, £9.00 to within the U.K.)

——, *Seventy times seven* Great Wakering, Mayhew McCrimmon, 1979, reprinted as *The Gift of Forgiveness*.

——, *The Gift of Forgiveness* by the Catholic Truth Society, London, 1983. Now out of print.

Sheed, Frank, *Theology and Sanity,* London, Sheed and Ward, 1948.

Staniforth, Maxwell (ed.), *Early Christian Writings,* Harmondsworth, Penguin Classics, 1968.

Teresa of Jesus, *The Interior Castle or The Mansions,* (ed. Zimmerman), London, Thomas Baker, 1912.

Tertullian, *The Writings of Tertullian,* tr. S. Thelwall, Edinburgh T. & T. Clark, 1869.

Todd, John M., *Martin Luther,* London, Burns and Oates, 1964.

Those of my own books marked with an asterisk may be obtained direct from me, as stocks are kept in Loyola Hall bookshop: prices given include postage to addresses within the UK. Send a cheque made out to LOYOLA HALL to the value stated, to Gerald O'Mahony, Loyola Hall, Warrington Road, Prescot, Merseyside L35 6NZ.

For further details see Web Page: www.loyolahall.co.uk.

Printed in the United Kingdom
by Lightning Source UK Ltd.
124263UK00001B/265-291/A